# SOARING

ISBN 0 948205 03 2

First published 1986 by
**White Line Press**
60 Bradford Road, Stanningley, Leeds,
LS28 6EF

This second edition, revised and updated, published 1989

**Photographs**: pages 44, 45, Trevor Birkbeck; all others by the author

Editing: Philip Gardner
Design: Gerald Rogers
Diagrams: Stephen Beaumont
Cartoons: Bill Rudling

Typeset in 10/11pt Plantin by Text Management Services, Huddersfield
Origination: Impression

Printed and bound in Great Britain



**Note**
Throughout this book, the pronouns 'he', 'him' and 'his' have been used inclusively, and are intended to apply to both men and women. It is important in sport, as elsewhere, that women and men should have equal status and equal opportunities.

## Dedication

For Robert, who learned to soar in less time than it took to write the book

# STARTING SOARING

A guide for the new hang-glider pilot

Noel Whittall

WHITE LINE PRESS

# CONTENTS

# INTRODUCTION

When the first edition of this book was written, the basic qualification for new hang-glider pilots in Britain was the old 'P1' certificate. This was very simple, and did not require the pupil to have any experience of soaring. The current P1+ (Club Pilot Certificate) is a little more comprehensive, and has introduced some soaring tasks. I hope that you will find this edition helpful both when you are trying to complete the soaring tasks under the eye of an Instructor or Club Coach and when you go on to fly relatively unsupervised.

The early stages of soaring can be very frustrating, and learning to temper enthusiasm with patience is always hard. The more you understand, the faster you will get results, and the safer you will be. Even though you are being guided by a Club Coach, don't get into the habit of letting someone else do your thinking for you.

*Starting Soaring* is intended to supplement authoritative manuals such as the BHGA's *Pilot Handbook* or more advanced publications, not to replace them. You must be aware of the rules of the air as they affect hang-glider pilots, and constantly take in information from other sources so that your knowledge keeps pace with your improving flying ability.

Let's get away from the idea that soaring is difficult. It is not. On a good site, on the right day, it is easier to soar and top-land than to fly down into a bottom landing field. The difficult part is getting to that good site at the right time, and *knowing* that the time is right. And that doesn't mean just the right time from the weather point of view—it has to be right for *you* as well, both mentally and physically.

Once you have left your training school, I am a firm believer in the 'one thing at a time' approach. For example, I don't consider that it is a good idea to make a serious attempt to soar before you have mastered the technique of flying fully prone. So it is not a waste of time or opportunity if you spend a perfectly soarable day flying from top to bottom while becoming familiar with getting into the stirrup and adjusting to the way the glider seems to feel slightly different when you are suspended completely above the control bar: you will have made an investment in skill which will greatly improve your likelihood of soaring really successfully on the next good day.

The ideas and suggestions given here are simply that: ideas and suggestions. No claim is made that they represent the only way to learn to fly well, or that every new pilot will need to employ each and every one of them. But I can guarantee that they have all been proved to work effectively.

Increase your knowledge by talking to other pilots and reading all you can about this new freedom to fly. Join the local club and enjoy the company of other people who share your love of adventure.

Above all, learn at your own speed and enjoy the learning. At this stage hang gliding should be a non-competitive activity. Don't get disheartened if other fliers seem to be progressing much faster than you. If you make a conscious effort to learn something extra from each flight you will be learning at the correct speed for *your* abilities—and that is what counts.

*It helps if you are confident enough to enjoy your first soaring.*

## Chapter 1

# THE RIGHT APPROACH

Mastering the art of soaring is really a straightforward matter of doing a number of fairly simple things in the right order. Perform any of the elements in a sloppy or halfhearted manner, and success will be hard to come by. Start off by resolving to master each stage progressively, with a safety-oriented but determined approach, and there will be few problems.

Like all types of flight, hang gliding requires a very positive mental attitude to safety. Some people have this instinctively, but most of us need to learn it to a greater or lesser extent. It is a lesson that men who fly have been learning ever since Icarus stuck his wings on with non-aircraft quality adhesives, and it has given rise to a number of aviation proverbs which have stood the test of time. They are no less valuable for their old age:

- Aviation in itself is not inherently dangerous, but it is extremely unforgiving of carelessness and stupidity.
- It's the ground that hurts!
- There are old pilots and bold pilots, but very very few old bold pilots.
- It is far better to be down here wishing you were up there, than up there wishing you were down here.

Right from the beginning you must cultivate your own judgement. It is necessary to learn to judge not only site and weather conditions, but also the quality of advice which you are given when you are out among other pilots. In the training school you *knew* that your teacher was qualified and would not let you fly in conditions you might not have been able to cope with. Out on the hill, it is rather different; other pilots who do not know you will often tend to overestimate your capabilities rather than underestimate them. Don't be afraid of telling people that you are a low-airtime pilot—then you will be more likely to get exactly the guidance you need.

Another point which is easily overlooked is the knack of asking the right questions. Remember, once you are in the air, all your mental energies will be fully occupied with flying your aircraft, and you can do without working out puzzles at this stage. Imagine you have asked before launch 'Is it OK to fly here?', and are told: 'Yes, but try not to land in that big field just over the wall.' You then may think that you have sufficient information to launch with confidence. You make a good take-off, and manage a couple of beats along the ridge before the doubts set in ... The air turns out to be much rougher than you had bargained for, and you very soon wish you were back on the ground again. You hang onto the bar with an alloy-crushing vice-grip, flying more and more erratically, while all the time the big field behaves like a giant green magnet. It seems the only safe and logical place to get down into. If only we were allowed to land in that lovely big field ... but, mindful of the experienced pilot's warning, you manage to avoid it, scraping in beside the wall all in a heap and at the cost of a bent upright.

The only sop to your pride is that you did at least land outside that field. Throughout your descent you had been wondering just why it was to be avoided: is it an area of glider-smashing rotor turbulence, or maybe the farmer shoots on sight? All sorts of unlikely reasons pass through your mind. Your flight would have been very different had you known that the regulars avoid it only because it means an inconvenient walk of a couple of hundred metres down to the gate to carry the glider out!

If you had simply asked the right questions at the beginning, there would have been no problems. In this case you really wanted to know where the safest landing areas are, not just a vague affirmation that it is OK to fly.

The finest training aid you can have is another pilot who can coach you as you progress. This person may be your club's official coach, it may be someone who is a BHGA appointed Observer, or possibly just a relatively mature flier whose judgement you can respect. Watch out for the character who wants to push you along at *his* speed rather than encouraging you to learn safely and progressively. Instincts of self preservation should make you wary of the type who says such things as 'Yeh, get lobbed off from the top: those old gliders need a bit of a blow to keep 'em up, and yer'll have plenty of space underneath yer boots to sort things out if it's a bit rough.' Although there is a germ of truth in the idea that height equates with safety, a rather more considered approach is desirable!

All the time you must progress at a speed which *you* can handle comfortably; you should not feel that you have to be attempting the same flights as others on the hill. Once you are away from the training slopes, you will probably be sharing the sites with people whose experience covers a very wide range indeed: some of the pilots around you at launch could well be world-class fliers. The opportunity to share the air with top-grade performers is an attractive feature of hang gliding; there is always the opportunity to learn from the best. But don't think you have to fly just because others do, and if it *is* safe for you to launch, don't be disheartened if your performance isn't as good as theirs —it all takes time!

A word about communication: it's difficult. You will find that it is no problem for people on the ground to hear what you shout down to them, because your words will be wind-assisted. The difficulty is in hearing what is being shouted up at you! More than one promising first soaring attempt has been ruined because the enthusiastic 'coach' has been bellowing unnecessary words of encouragement which have at best been half heard by the pupil: it is very easy for a pilot who is exploring the strange world of lift for the first time to assume that the little shouting figure jumping up and down on the hill-edge is warning of previously unimagined dangers.

In this situation it may be useful if the coach has a loud-hailer, but it would have to be used very sparingly. Better, I think, to rely on really thorough pre-flight question sessions and subsequent de-briefings rather than for the coach to attempt to load you up with extra instructions in the air.

It is possible to employ ground-to-air CB radio (the reverse is not legal), but don't rely on it. You can bet that as soon as there is an important message for the coach to convey to you, your channel will be invaded by garrulous pensioners or love-lorn schoolkids.

In any case, be sure that you *understand* why you will be attempting a particular flight pattern and landing approach: give your coach or helper both the questions and your answers. You want him to confirm that your judgement is right, rather than simply to give instructions which you only half understand, yet follow blindly.

Remember, no matter how much help and guidance you receive from others, hang gliding is an intensely personal sport. The decision to fly must always be yours and yours alone. It is not possible to experience the amazing freedom which flight gives without being aware of the responsibility which is inseparable from it.

*The Super Scorpion: a design of the 1970s which became a favourite, but is now rather dated. Note the safety wheels on the control bar—a confidence booster in your early days.*

## Checklist

- Cultivate your own judgement.
- Think about the questions you ask.
- Find a reliable senior pilot, and respect the advice you are given.
- Attempt only one new thing at a time.

# Chapter 2
# CHOOSING THE RIGHT GLIDER

Your first hang glider will represent a substantial investment in your new sport, so it is worth taking the trouble to ensure that what you buy will suit your needs in the best possible way. The finest advice that you, the new pilot, can have is not to buy a glider on your own—you need the help of someone with up-to-date experience of the market.

You will hear gliders referred to according to their 'generation'. Do not consider buying anything earlier than fourth generation (see over).

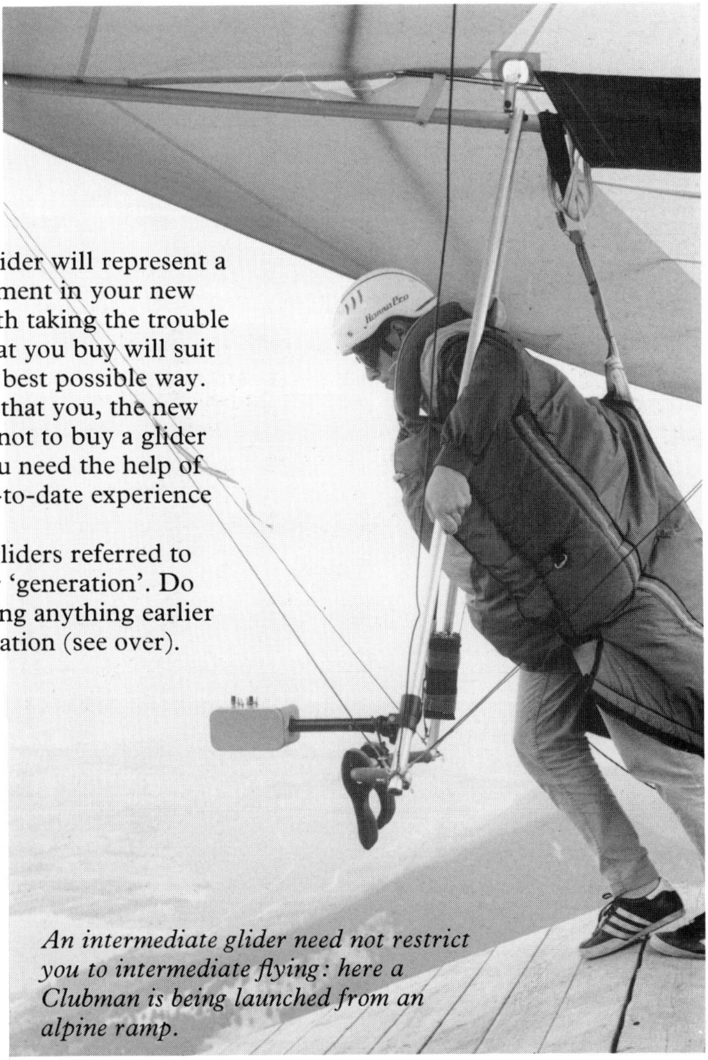

*An intermediate glider need not restrict you to intermediate flying: here a Clubman is being launched from an alpine ramp.*

## Obsolete models

You should avoid old gliders for the good reason that they are simply not as safe as those built after 1978–1979. We did not know so much about the aerodynamics of flexible-winged aircraft in the early days, and standards of design were much lower. The most important feature a glider needs is good pitch stability, and this was not always guaranteed on gliders built in the 1970s.

Of course, sheer age alone is also a perfectly good reason to reject any glider. The sailcloth does eventually deteriorate, and aluminium does corrode.

Unless a glider has been stored under exceptionally good conditions and little used, it will probably be near the end of its useful life after about seven years, and its resale value correspondingly low. Those which have spent much of their flying time in the salt-laden atmosphere of coastal sites may suffer from airframe corrosion which can have shortened their lives to considerably less than the average elsewhere. There is no such thing as a glider which is 'fairly safe', or 'OK if you don't go too high'. An aircraft is either fit to fly or fit for scrap: there is no in-between stage!

*Three classic intermediate gliders*: left to right, *Super Scorpion, Cherokee and Atlas. The first two are now obsolete, but the Atlas remains a favourite throughout the world.*

## Fourth-generation and purpose-built intermediate gliders

The gliders mentioned here all have a blend of handling and performance which makes them particularly suitable for the new pilot. They do not all have the BHGA's Certificate of Airworthiness, often because they are old designs produced by companies which have gone out of business. Some, such as the Atlas and Polaris, have equivalent foreign certification. Others are only certified in a

particular size. My advice is always to buy a fully certified glider if at all possible: you know that it is safe, and need not fear being grounded by a bureaucrat who may, at some future time, decide to restrict flying to certified gliders only.

Lists of gliders with approval are published regularly in the BHGA magazine. Information on foreign gliders can be obtained from the BHGA office.

*Fourth-generation* indicates a stage in the evolution of the hang glider marked by the introduction of the 'Atlas' design from the French La Mouette company. It is characterised by a deep area of double surface at the leading edge of the wing, and sail battens which are permanently curved to the airfoil shape. This combination has produced a glider with very good all-round performance.

*Purpose-built intermediates* covers models bearing a strong family resemblance to the Atlas, such as the successful Italian-built Polaris 'Delta', as well as more sophisticated types with a larger area of double-surfaced wing. A typical example is the original Aerial Arts 'Clubman' with exposed cross-tubes. And although it defies exact classification, the Goldmarque 'Gyr' falls within this general category too.

Here are some comments on gliders in this grouping which you are likely to find on the British market:

## Atlas

Excellent minimum-sink performance makes it easy to stay high in ridge lift. Nicely co-ordinated handling, but

*The Atlas is likely to remain a classic intermediate glider for many years.*

noticeably slow to respond in roll if you are at the bottom end of the recommended weight range for the size you are flying. Spares are available in the UK, but the use of metric tube sizes can cause delays.

## Clubman 1

The Brighton-built Clubman range are lightweight machines with some innovative design features, built with the intermediate pilot in mind. Responsive handling and good performance at medium speed. The original model with exposed cross-tubes was soon superseded by the enclosed version, so see also the 'Clubman CFX' in the next section.

## Cutlass

Skyhook Sailwings' 'Cutlass' is a rugged and simple glider with very forgiving flying characteristics. A thoroughly sound choice for a first soaring glider. No longer in production, its replacement is the 'Gipsy' from the same company.

*The characteristic wing planform of the Gyr shows well here.*

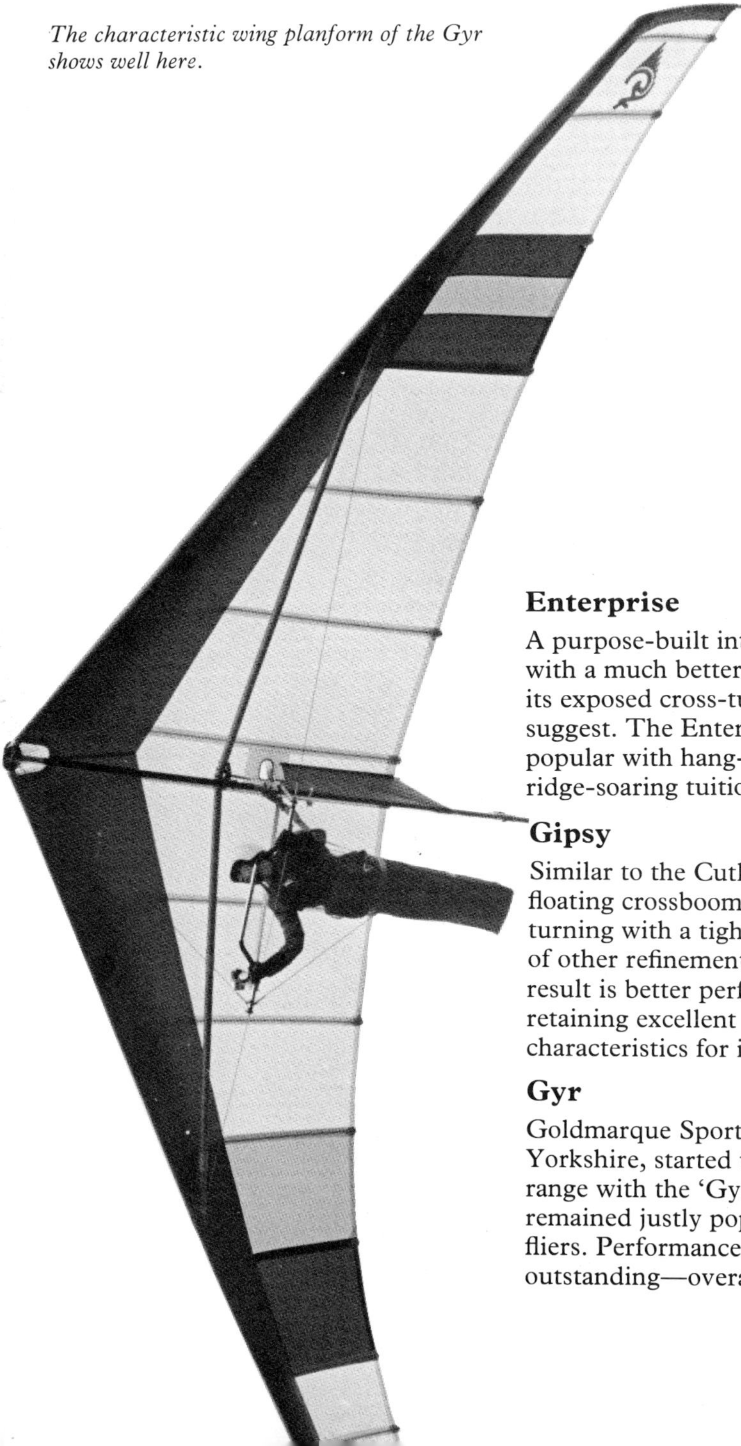

**Enterprise**

A purpose-built intermediate glider with a much better glide-angle than its exposed cross-tubes would suggest. The Enterprise is especially popular with hang-gliding schools for ridge-soaring tuition.

**Gipsy**

Similar to the Cutlass, but with a floating crossboom to give easier turning with a tighter sail, plus a host of other refinements. The overall result is better performance while retaining excellent handling characteristics for intermediate pilots.

**Gyr**

Goldmarque Sports, from East Yorkshire, started their production range with the 'Gyr', and it has remained justly popular among club fliers. Performance is outstanding—overall possibly the best in this category. The Gyr has a wide nose angle, which results in a greater wingspan than the rest of the intermediates, and it looks as if it would be a bit of a handful because of this. Appearances, however, are deceptive, and the glider is very easy to handle in the air, although maybe a little extra care or some assistance is needed to keep the wings level just prior to launch. The Gyr is immensely strong, but rather heavy. That is not a problem if you learn to soar and top-land on accessible sites, but if you contemplate lots of carrying-up it doesn't help!

## Hilander

This was an Atlas-type model from Flexiform Skysails. Not many were made, and I have never flown one, but respected pilots rate its suitability quite highly.

*The BHGA's test rig about to test a Storm for pitch stability. Not many pre-1980 gliders have been tested in this way—something to be borne in mind when considering the purchase of an older model.*

## Mega 2

Moyes Gliders, the parent company of which is in Australia, are renowned worldwide. Enough examples of this model have found their way to the UK for it to be worth including in this list. Some were built here under licence, some in Spain, some in Italy, and some in the USA, so there may be differences in detail or tube specification which should be borne in mind if the prospect of spares or repairs may become important. A super performer which makes a good budget buy. Strong but heavy, so the comments on the Gyr also apply.

## Polaris 'Delta'

Built in a modern factory in Italy, the Polaris 'Delta' is very popular throughout Europe. Of the Atlas style, and with very high quality detail work, it is chosen by many recreational pilots in the Alps in preference to later, faster-landing types. The speed range is actually very good for a glider which has no pretentions as a racer, while the rate of turn is excellent. At the time of writing secondhand Polarises are keenly sought after, so it is easy to change to a higher-performance glider without losing much money.

## Fifth-generation CFX gliders

CFX stands for 'concealed floating crossboom', and this feature is characteristic of the fifth generation of modern hang gliders. The advantage of this type is that they are 'cleaner' aerodynamically, and so can generate more lift by flying faster, which results in a comparatively flat glide angle. Once you are a proficient and

# HOW TO BUY YOUR FIRST HANG GLIDER

GET A GLIDER YOU CAN CARRY, THERE'S A LOT OF CARRYING IN THE EARLY DAYS.
The CLUBMAN is the lightest glider around.

GET THE RIGHT SIZE GLIDER TO SUIT YOUR WEIGHT. SOME GLIDERS ONLY COME IN "MR. AVERAGE" SIZE.
The CLUBMAN comes in three sizes, one to suit you.

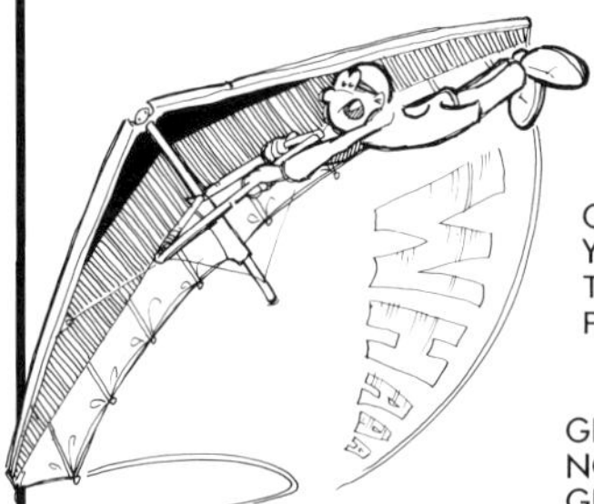

GET AN EASY TO FLY GLIDER. IT WILL BOOST YOUR CONFIDENCE AND ABILITY.
The CLUBMAN is widely accepted as the best P1 glider.

GET A GLIDER DESIGNED FOR THE NEW PILOT. DO NOT BE TEMPTED BY "AN OLD SECOND HAND GLIDER". IT MAY BE TOTALLY UNACCEPTABLE AND DIFFICULT TO RE-SELL.
The CLUBMAN'S second hand value is legendary and a year's careful flying can be surprisingly cheap.

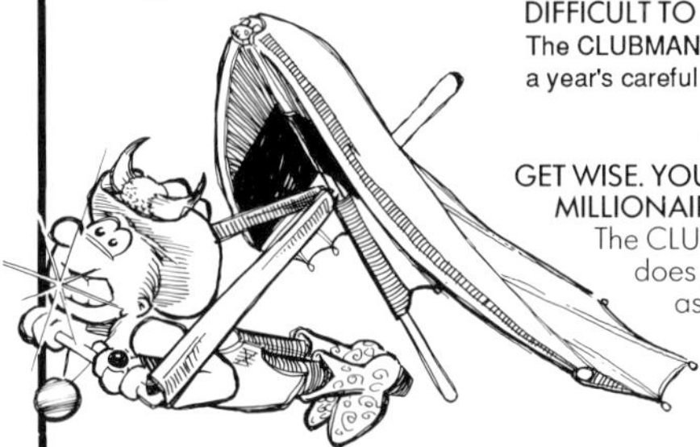

GET WISE. YOU DO NOT HAVE TO BE A TEXAN MILLIONAIRE TO OWN A GOOD GLIDER.
The CLUBMAN is not the most expensive, but it does represent the best value you can buy, ask any CLUBMAN owner.

GET A SECOND OPINION. IT MAY SAVE YOU A LOT MORE THAN JUST MONEY.

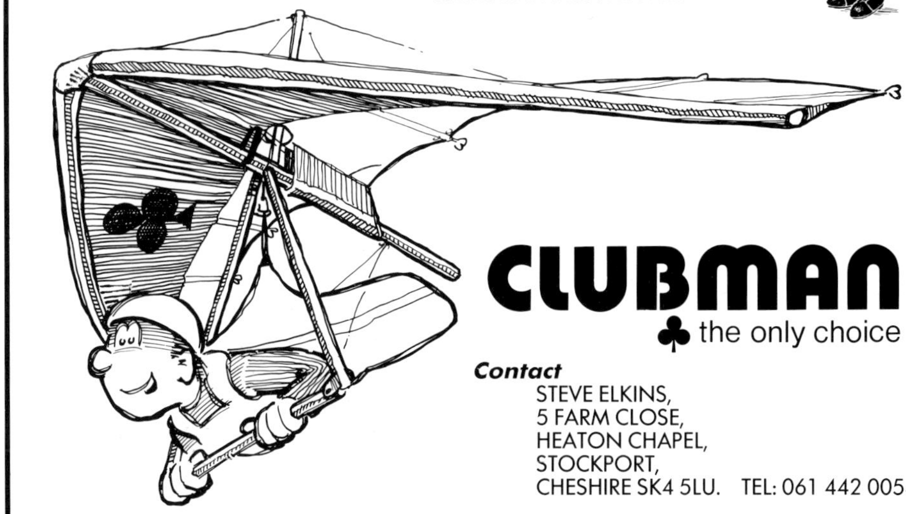

CLUBMAN

♣ the only choice

**Contact**

STEVE ELKINS,
5 FARM CLOSE,
HEATON CHAPEL,
STOCKPORT,
CHESHIRE SK4 5LU. TEL: 061 442 0054

The Clubman C160 is BHGA approved. CoA pending on all other models.

confident pilot, this is a great adavantage, but in the early stages it is a mixed blessing—particularly when trying to judge landing approaches. However, some CFX models are designed with the less experienced flier in mind, and these are good aircraft on which to do your first soaring. The others tend to be rather heavy, which makes them harder to cope with at all stages on the ground, and particularly just after touchdown.

Listed below are most of the current CFXs, with my personal comments on what I think of their suitability for first soaring. I am not saying that it is impossible to go on to any of them direct from P1: however, with the exception of the first three on the list, you will certainly find progress less daunting and enjoy yourself a lot more if you first spend a few months flying a glider from the previous group.

## Fifth-generation gliders built with beginners in mind

*Calypso*

It took Airwave, manufacturers of the highly-successful 'Magic' range of gliders, a long time to make a model which was suitable for the intermediate pilot. The Calypso is their offering, and is proving highly successful. Developed from the same original US design as the Vision, the Calypso is entirely British made, and is easily identified by its lack of a keel pocket.

*Clubman CFX*

Designed as a high-performance intermediate, but taking advantage of CFX technology, this is a very good choice for the ambitious beginner. As well as being easy to rig, its remarkably light weight (only 46 lb for the 140 sq ft model!) makes it easy to carry and control on the ground.

*Vision*

The 'Vision' is an American design of sail fitted onto British hardware at the Hiway factory. A wide range of adjustment is provided, which allows initial flights to be made in a very 'soft' state of tune for stable handling—a good arrangement which permits the glider to be tuned to match your growing abilities. When tightened up, the performance should satisfy virtually any recreational flier. The Vision is another lightweight at 55 lb.

*Zeus*

A conscious effort by Len Gabriels of Skyhook Sailwings to make a lightweight CFX with sweet handling. Good-quality workmanship with nice details such as zippered inspection panels. The result should not provide any problems for a competent P1. A little heavier than the Vision, but still very manageable.

*A Clubman CFX above the Yorkshire Dales.*

## Other fifth-generation models

Since 1981 these have become the usual type of hang glider seen on the hills. Most of them owe a lot to the original Ultralight Products 'Comet' design, and in moderately experienced hands offer delightful flying. There are plenty to be bought secondhand at reasonable prices and no doubt many new pilots will master them reasonably well. However, I still have no hesitation in repeating that I think you will have a more enjoyable time if you fly an easier glider from the previous lists for the first few months.

*Azur*

From La Mouette in France. I found roll-effort rather high.

*Comet*

Built in England under licence from the UP factory in the USA. Nice to fly, but the very slack side-wires feel strange to relatively inexperienced pilots, particularly when steadying the glider prior to launch.

*Demon*

A product of the original Hiway firm. Excellent handling in the air, but hard work on the ground. Also has a reputation for flying on further in ground-effect than its contemporaries, which makes short-field landings rather tricky.

*Excalibur*

From the new Hiway company which also produces the Vision. Easily identified by its curved tips. I found the 'Excalibur' pleasant to fly, but definitely not a 'post-P1' glider. The Vision is a far better bet to learn to soar on.

*Javelin*

A high-performance glider from Goldmarque Sports. Not for beginners.

*Magic range*

The latest 'Magic' is often the choice of serious competition pilots the world over. Wait until you have developed the skill to do it justice, and then consider investing in a model one, three or four, according to the depth of your pocket.

The Airwave company which produces the Magics did make a small number of intermediate gliders, called the 'Wizard'. Only three or four reached the public, so your chances of finding one are slight, but if you do, it will serve very nicely!

*Sabre*

Skyhook Sailwings' first full CFX model. Relatively docile compared with some, but feels a bit of a handful to the uninitiated.

*Shadow*

Another Goldmarque glider. I enjoyed flying it, but the rapidity with which it accelerates when you pull speed on could cause problems for the inexperienced.

*Typhoon range*

Like the Magics, the Typhoons are favoured by competition fliers of many nations, and the same comments apply. That is not to imply that either of these ranges are exclusively competition gliders, but they do generally have more weight and high-speed capability than you are going to need for a few months yet.

This list is far from complete, but it covers most of the gliders you will come across on the UK market. Fortunately there is a trend towards producing more models suitable for the intermediate market, so watch the advertisements in the magazines.

## Where do I buy a glider?

At this stage in your flying, almost everyone else knows more about hang gliders than you do, so you need advice. It makes sense to consult your instructor, who will have the best idea of the type which will suit your abilities the best. Most schools deal in new and secondhand wings, and you can be sure that if they are approved by the BHGA, any glider you buy from them will be in a safe and sound condition. The modest extra you should expect to pay when buying from a professional is good value when you realise that your glider will have been properly inspected and correctly tuned by someone who stands to lose his school registration and thus his livelihood if he passes on an unsound machine.

Of course you can also find good gliders for sale in the clubs or privately. Be a little more wary of those advertised in national non-specialist magazines or local papers. This is where the faded old relics which have had a hard life often end up: really good gliders are usually sold inside the sport. If you are tempted by an apparent bargain, first check out with an experienced flier that it isn't a model with a really poor reputation, and then add on a few pounds to cover the cost of having it stripped and inspected by a dealer or the manufacturer. If the manufacturer is no longer in business, there may be a good reason why! The BHGA is always happy to advise on glider suitability, and publishes an annual update in the springtime training issue of its magazine, *Wings!*.

In any case, get any secondhand machine properly checked *before* you use it. This may not seem quite so important when you are really keen to make your first flight with it, but you will find that when you are hanging under the thing several hundred feet up in the sky, there are segments of your consciousness which will focus on every creak and groan the airframe produces. At that point a checkout will have seemed a very good investment indeed.

## Size and tune and trim

A glider which is the wrong size for you will certainly spoil your enjoyment of flight, even if it doesn't turn out to be downright dangerous. If it is too large, you will find it extremely difficult to turn, and it will lack penetration in high winds. Too small, and it will be reluctant to gain height in ridge lift, and also the landing speed will be high. All the manufacturers publish the pilot weight range for which their particular models are suitable, but don't forget that the figure given is your weight when you *clip in*, rather than when you stand stripped on the bathroom scales.

The performance of most gliders can be influenced considerably by their state of tune: for example, tightening the sail will usually improve the glide angle, but at the expense of the ease of turning. As a beginner, it is the handling which is of prime importance to you, and you need your wing in a 'soft' state of tune. A reputable dealer will set the glider up correctly for your skill level, but this may not be the case if you buy privately. This is yet another good reason to have any secondhand purchase competently inspected before flying it.

Trim is slightly different from tune: with your hands off the bar, the glider should be trimmed to fly straight and level, safely above stalling speed. No two gliders are identical in this respect, and the same glider will behave differently with different weights of pilot aboard. For example, a heavier pilot will load the airframe more, which allows more *twist* in the sail: in turn this has the effect of increasing the *angle of attack* at which the aircraft flies, and thus slows its flight at any given bar position. Bear in mind that the stall speed rises as the pilot weight increases, and you can see that this effect could mislead an inexperienced pilot who relies on bar-position alone to indicate speed-to-fly. In this example the heavier pilot should move the hang-point forward a little in order to re-trim the glider, which is the opposite of what would be required if we were considering a non-flexible wing. Adjusting gliders is a delicate business, so unless you are following specific instructions in the manufacturer's handbook, leave tuning and trimming to experts.

Gliders often show a slight tendency to turn in one direction, and need to be trimmed to fly straight. The most likely reason is uneven sail tension, which is not too difficult to adjust. However, it is always wise to have the leading edge tubes removed and rolled on a flat surface to check whether there is a slight bend or 'set' in either of them, as that almost guarantees a turn. Needless to say, a bent tube should be replaced. It is essential that the airframe is stripped and inspected carefully if the amount of adjustment needed results in a noticeable difference in the position of the sail on the leading edges.

## Battens

Unlike most training-school gliders, your intermediate or CFX model will use the pre-formed aluminium type of batten. These demand an extra degree of care and attention: you must regularly check that they still follow the airfoil shape which the manufacturer intended. Make sure that you get a set of profile drawings with any glider you buy.

It is a good habit to check the battens of one wing against those of the other each time you rig—only a slight difference will put a persistent turn into the wing. Watch out also that you don't snag a wingtip when ground-handling prior to launch: the effect of a bent tip-batten can be quite dramatic!

*Battens have to be inspected carefully each time you fly ...*

*... and a little adjustment made if necessary.*

Sometimes a batten can snag in its pocket when trying to draw it out. This can be quite a problem on some CFX models, and various remedies are possible. *None of them involves the use of force!* First try pushing the batten right home again, and then pull and twist slightly at the same time. If the sail is untensioned, re-tension it and try pulling the batten with the sail tight, just far enough to clear the snag (I know that this works on my own glider). Sometimes an extra pair of hands is needed, to push the forward end up from underneath, while you continue to pull. Be patient, because sail repairs within the double surface are expensive.

## Checklist

- Get expert advice when buying your first soaring glider.
- Choose a fourth-generation model, or one of the specially-designed intermediate CFX types.
- Be sure it is not in too high a state of tune for your skill level.
- Get the trim checked by someone of similar weight to yourself.
- Realise that the battens have to be maintained carefully.

## Chapter 3
# EQUIPMENT

### Your harness

So often the novice pilot will spend as much as possible on the glider, and yet not budget enough for a decent harness. This doesn't make sense, because a good harness will last you for more seasons than will your first wing—always provided that you buy a comfortable one initially.

For some years, the enclosed style of harness was looked on as being suitable for experienced pilots only, but recent experience has shown that they can be used successfully by novices also. These 'Supp' or 'Pod' models, all based on the original Keller design, are fine, *provided that you take the trouble to learn how to use them properly, and always check that your legs are in the leg-loops before each flight*.

For the first dozen flights, it is best to remove the zip and the cord which operates the 'bomb doors' (the zip is usually only held in with velcro), and simply place your feet on the internal stirrup. I recommend removing the cord completely, because it is all too easy to get your leg tangled up in it when you first come out of the prone position.

Once you are really confident, you can refit the zip, and try operating it in flight. Then unzip immediately; until you are a polished flier, you don't want to have to think about unzipping at the same time as you are setting up your final approach.

The lower cost and lack of bulk of the stirrup harness still make it the usual choice for a pilot who is starting soaring. They are simple to get into and out of, and can be very comfortable if they fit properly and are carefully adjusted. Try the following tips:

The ideal way to test a harness before purchase is to try it out while hanging in front of a large mirror, but unfortunately this is rarely possible. The most important feature to check is the position of the main lifting straps. These are the ones that rise up from each side in the region of the hips. They govern both the ease with which your body rotates into the prone position on launch, and the comfort of the position in flight. If the harness is basically too short for you, you will feel leg-heavy. Attempts to adjust it will result in the whole apron coming too far down your body, and you will end up with your shoulders resting on straps rather than on the padded parts designed for the purpose. Too long a harness is more hazardous: if you try to make it fit by shortening the stirrup ropes, excessive weight will be put onto the upper part of your body, and while getting into prone will be simplicity itself, getting out again will be quite a different matter!

If you find the approximate balance point of your body by lying with your hips across a beam or gate, and then check that the main lift straps join the apron within a centimetre or so of that point, you should not have much trouble getting the rest of the adjustments right. A friend is needed for this: the traditional method is to suspend

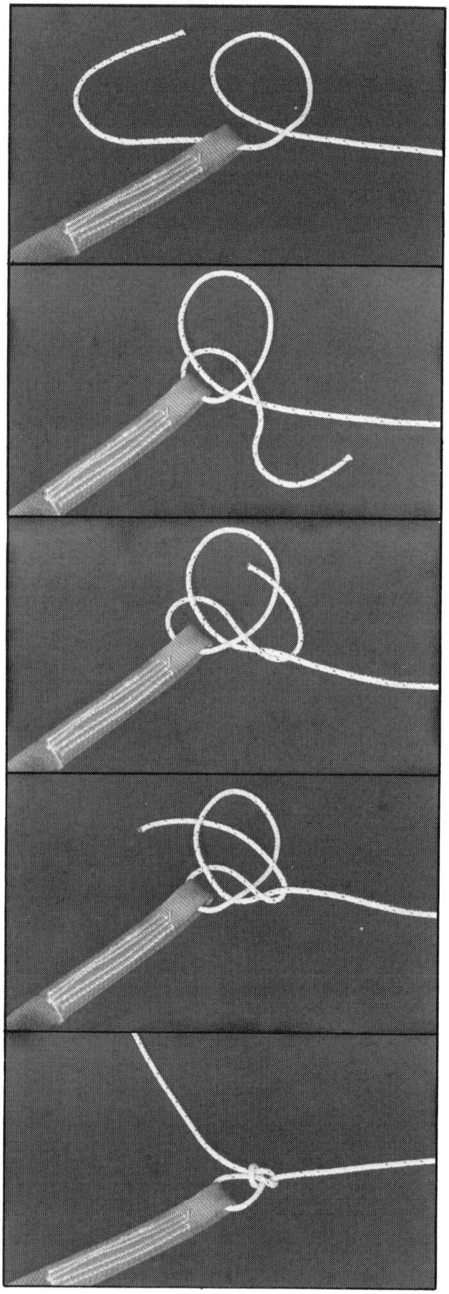

*The bowline is the knot to use when adjusting the length of harness lines.*

yourself in the harness from a strong point in a garage or similar while your helper checks the straps and cords for tension, and alters them as necessary. The object is to get your weight distributed as evenly as possible *when in your flying attitude.* Ideally it is desirable to be truly horizontal, but if this feels excessively strange, and you think that having your head a few centimetres higher than your feet for the first few flights would make life easier, then that's OK too.

Time spent hanging in your new harness is not wasted. If you rig up a dummy control bar, you can get used to the full-prone position and practise moving your weight without twisting your body or letting your legs swing sideways. After a few minutes you will experience the exquisite pain which a bunch of car keys and a handful of small change can inflict on the thighs if left in the trouser pockets. Less fortunate pilots wait until their first long flight to discover this ...

Some fliers advocate the use of the 'knee-hanger' type of harness for beginners because no stirrup is required. In my experience that is the only advantage, and it is far outweighed by the tendency of this type to restrict your ability to lift the control bar high enough to run well at take-off and touch-down. The resulting gibbon-like lope does have a certain entertainment value. Although they are still quite popular in the USA and Germany I think that knee-

*A simple elastic ankle loop is best.*

hangers are best avoided, particularly as getting into a stirrup is simplicity itself, as will be revealed!

## The dreaded stirrup

About ten years ago, on more or less the same day that the stirrup harness was invented, it was discovered that it was not always easy to locate with your feet a small piece of aluminium tube swinging around on ropes. It was extra difficult when the rest of you was engaged upon the newly-discovered activity of coaxing a hang glider into the air. A remedy was soon found in the form of a loop of elastic locating the stirrup behind one ankle. This was simple and effective, but for some reason also got a reputation for being a bit sissy, and such loops were usually referred to as 'nonk rubbers'. The result is that the macho types are still to be seen pedalling about the sky trying to curl their mud-encrusted boots around that elusive stirrup, while we sissies don't have any trouble at all.

The illustrations show the simplest type of ankle loop. The rubber should not be too tight—it needs to be able to ride up the leg quite easily. Note also that the diameter of the stirrup tube itself is smaller than usually supplied. This $\frac{5}{8}$-in tube of similar gauge seems to me a great improvement on the heavy $1\frac{1}{8}$-in material often used: not only is it less

*The loop should not fit too tightly around the leg.*

of a nuisance if it bangs against the legs while running, it also seems to locate the feet more readily without slipping.

The technique for finding the stirrup is straightforward, and very soon becomes instinctive. The only thing you have to remember is that your feet must operate on the 'first in last out' principle. If the loop is on your left leg, then it is the right foot which finds the stirrup every time. As you prepare to land, the right foot remains in the stirrup while the left moves forward and down through the loop again; finally you take the right foot off when your body is fully upright. The beauty of this system is that the stirrup is still located as it was for launch, so that in the event of having to overshoot on a top landing it is just as easy to regain the stirrup.

*See how a 'step-in' loop can easily foul around instrument mountings if it is held like this for take-off. I prefer to remove this sort of extra altogether and rely on the simple ankle loop.*

I make no claims that this is the *only* system which works, but I do guarantee that it works well. The only time I have ever known it to give any trouble was when flying in 'moon boots': the loop may sometimes ride up over the top of these fat boots, and it can then be a problem to get it down again.

Some pilots stiffen the stirrup ropes by running them through a couple of lengths of flexible plastic tubing, which prevents any chance of them tangling.

One type of extra which I am not at all keen on is the addition of a secondary loop of rope *under* the stirrup, which is supposed to form a sort of rung into which you first step. This method depends on the stirrup being in front of the legs at take-off, and the extra loop can be low enough to be in the way. If you hold it up against the control frame as you start your run, there is a chance of it catching on instrument mountings, with disastrous results. This really has happened—see illustration. Lastly, users of this method seem in general to be the greatest offenders when it comes to looking down at the stirrup during those critical moments just after launch.

## Other equipment

Remembering that we are talking only of your first soaring flights here, the rest of your equipment should be kept as simple as possible: the less there is, the less you have to think about, so that you can just concentrate on getting the flying right. Even if you have bought a super-bargain variometer or altimeter, leave it on the ground until you can fly well enough to spare the time to look at it. At this stage you should be more concerned with the basics like being warm and comfortable in the air!

## Clothing

### Oversuits

From your experience at the training school you will have discovered that even on a summer day the wind on the hills can be surprisingly cool. As soon as you become successful at soaring, you will be spending quite a lot of time flying into that wind, but without the heat-generating bursts of energy required to carry the glider back to the top. Investing in a one-piece oversuit of heavy cotton is really worthwhile even if it is only an industrial boilersuit. I particularly like the 'Protec' fully zippered suit which is a slimmed-down version of a parachuting outfit, now manufactured especially for hang gliding.

Whatever you wear, make sure that the action of putting your harness on doesn't pull your shirt away from your trousers, leaving a freezing gap around the kidneys—a very common occurrence.

In winter, an oversuit is a must. Fortunately winter sports have been responsible for the development of plenty of suitable warm gear. Ski and snowmobile wear are fine, while the 'Ozee' insulated suits with ankle-to-neck zips have become almost the

*Cool around the kidneys! It is easy for your harness to pull your shirt and jacket up at the back like this: a one-piece suit is the answer.*

standard winter wear for serious pilots. Condensation is always a problem, and a suit which allows ventilation without having to be completely removed is an advantage. The range of clothing incorporating 'breathing' linings such as 'Gore-tex' looks ideal, but the price can be a problem.

### Boots

Although many experienced fliers simply use trainers, tough boots certainly do lessen the danger of foot and ankle injury. The prime consideration is a sole pattern giving good grip. Avoid the type with an almost smooth sole and no break between sole and heel: they can slip

even on dry grass, and also make location of the stirrup difficult in flight. If your boots use hooks for the laces, either get them replaced with eyelets, or at least close them up. This is because the hooks have been known to snag around the rear rigging wires of the glider when in prone flight, causing loss of control.

### Gloves

Thin leather gloves are ideal for summer use, but in winter you will need something more substantial. Again, the ski-wear industry provides a wide choice. Once you have gained a little soaring experience a pair of those warm mitts which fit permanently on the control bar will provide the answer to cold fingers, but for first soaring you can do without any extra distractions like having to wriggle your hands into mitts at the start of your flight.

## Safety equipment

### Karabiners

The karabiner is the link between you and the glider. Cases of failure are almost unknown, and the type normally used will support a load of at least ten times the weight of the average pilot. However, the consequences of a failure are so serious that many pilots prefer to use two. An independent hang loop acting as a backup is also a comfort which you will appreciate when you get really high.

*Winter flying can be enjoyable if you have plenty of warm clothes.*

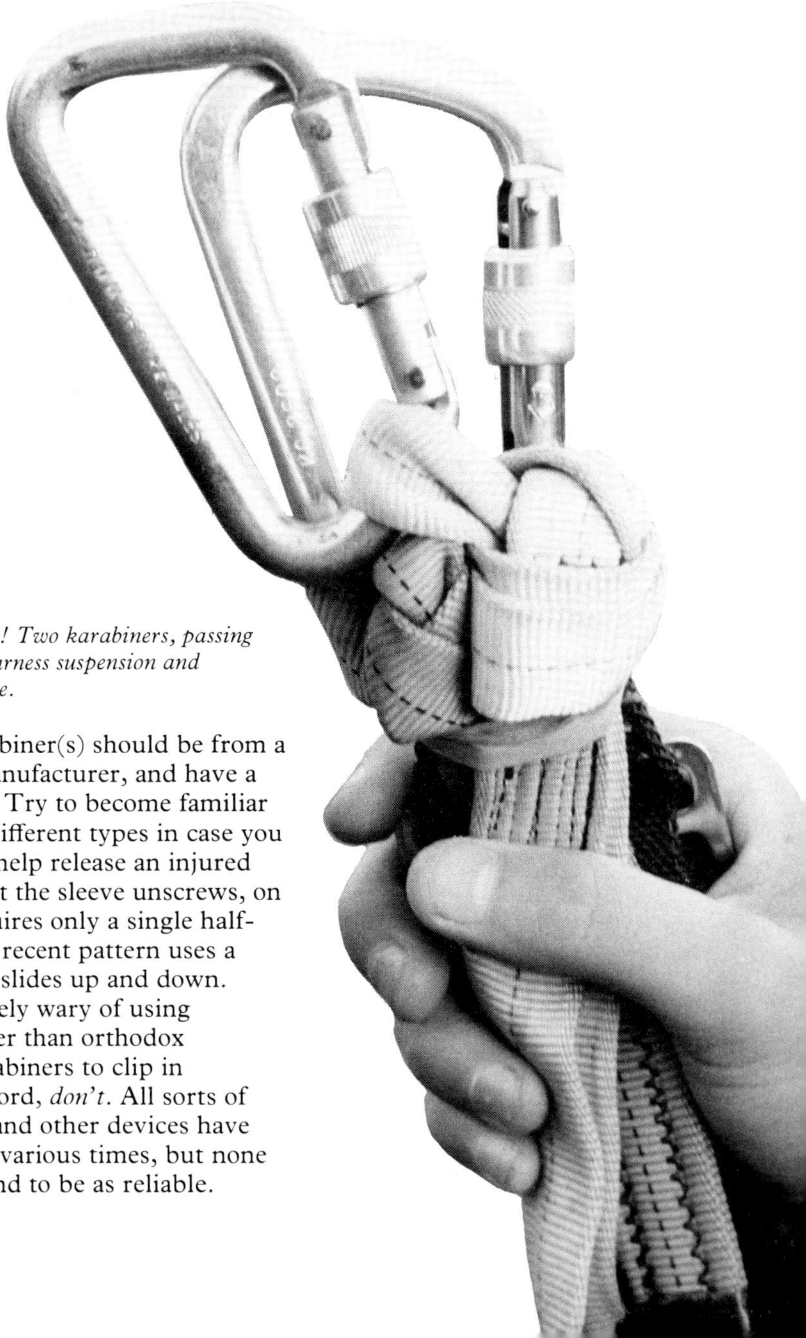

*Belt and braces! Two karabiners, passing through both harness suspension and parachute bridle.*

Your karabiner(s) should be from a reputable manufacturer, and have a locking gate. Try to become familiar with all the different types in case you ever have to help release an injured pilot: on most the sleeve unscrews, on others it requires only a single half-turn, while a recent pattern uses a sleeve which slides up and down.

Be extremely wary of using anything other than orthodox climbing karabiners to clip in with—in a word, *don't*. All sorts of cargo hooks and other devices have been tried at various times, but none has been found to be as reliable.

## Parachutes

An emergency parachute is a piece of equipment which any pilots who are serious about their sport or their necks should consider buying. Even as low as a couple of hundred feet, these devices have saved lives, and you will be getting to that sort of height very early on in your soaring career. The type of emergency which may demand a parachute deployment to get you back on the ground safely is exceptionally rare: the most probable reason could be a mid-air collision on a crowded site.

Carrying a parachute can also provide a psychological help to the new soaring pilot: I have come across more than one who has learned to soar quite easily, but then 'sticks' at ten-minute flights at a relatively low level, even when conditions are exceptionally good. This is not too surprising really—after all there is a lot of exposure up there, and once you have got over the initial stage of handling the glider, you have time to think about the enormity of what you are doing, and start to worry about it. Simply carrying a parachute can provide the extra sense of security you need to help you through this not uncommon phase. Beware though of going to the other extreme and becoming over-confident once you have one.

If possible, invest in a new 'chute—they last for many years with care. Make sure that it is properly fitted to your harness or glider, depending on type. (The glider-mounted models are very unusual now, being almost entirely confined to microlight aircraft use.) The parachute should come with packing instructions, and you must make yourself familiar with the method of deployment.

Secondhand parachutes do occasionally come onto the market, and should be purchased with as much care as your first glider—your life may depend on it! Never part with money without seeing the canopy fully opened and re-packed, and take particular care to check that it has been stored in dry conditions. Mildew is an obvious enemy, but so also is sunlight: check carefully for signs of discoloration which could be due to ultraviolet radiation or chemical attack.

When you get out to the hill for the first time with your new parachute, you will have to make an extra-careful hang check. If you have bought one of the more normal chest-mounted systems, your harness-height may need shortening a little so that there is no danger of the parachute pack touching the bar in flight. You must *always* check that the container is properly closed before launching, whatever the type of system. If your model uses a pin to keep the container closed, include checking this in your pre-flight routine. If yours is a secondhand model, inspect with great care any Velcro which keeps the container closed: it doesn't retain its efficiency for ever, and accidental deployments are not only far too common, they are also potentially very serious. Replace tired Velcro!

All parachutes need to be correctly re-packed at regular intervals, every three months being the ideal.

Look upon the purchase of a

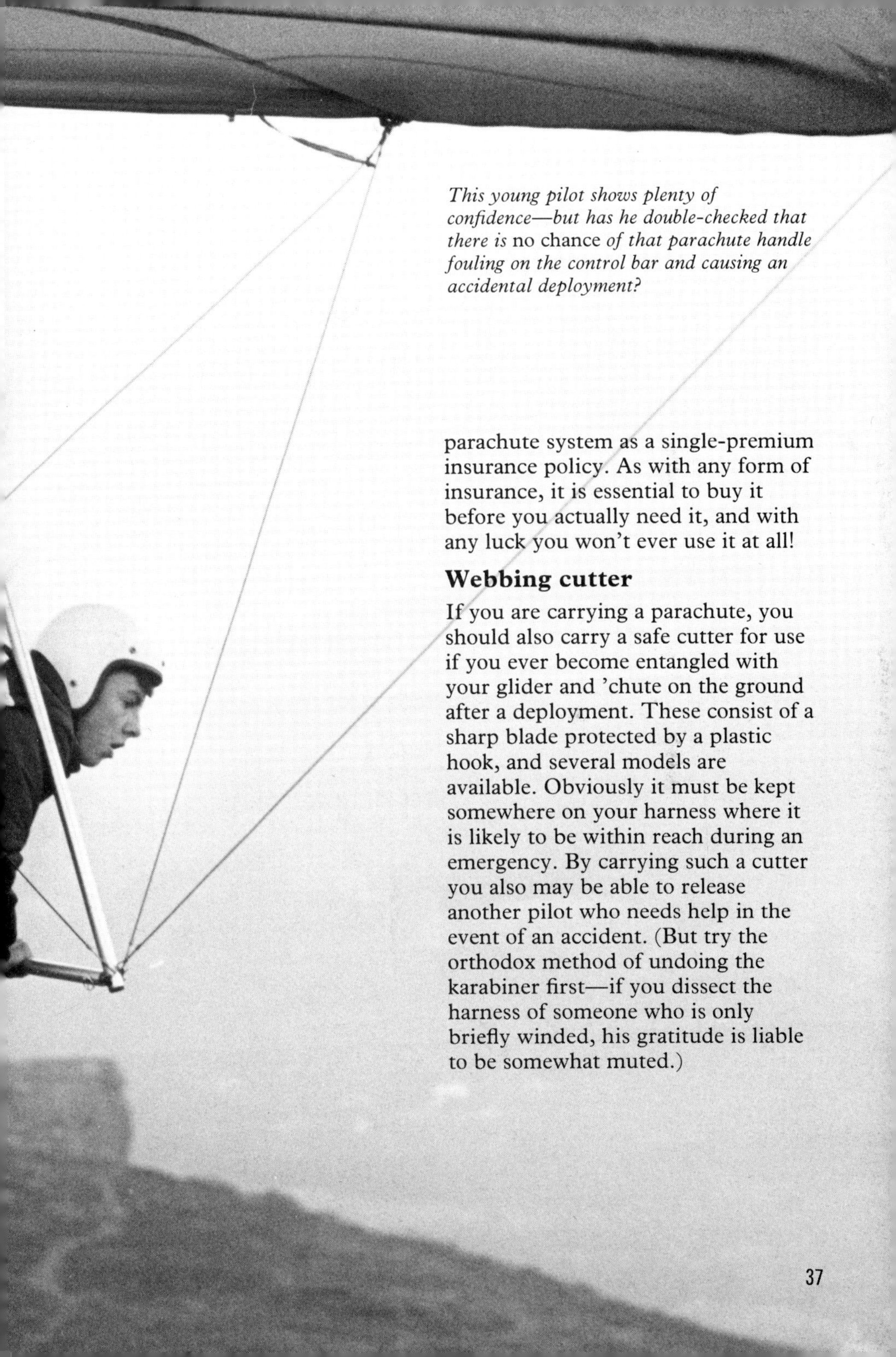

*This young pilot shows plenty of confidence—but has he double-checked that there is* no chance *of that parachute handle fouling on the control bar and causing an accidental deployment?*

parachute system as a single-premium insurance policy. As with any form of insurance, it is essential to buy it before you actually need it, and with any luck you won't ever use it at all!

## Webbing cutter

If you are carrying a parachute, you should also carry a safe cutter for use if you ever become entangled with your glider and 'chute on the ground after a deployment. These consist of a sharp blade protected by a plastic hook, and several models are available. Obviously it must be kept somewhere on your harness where it is likely to be within reach during an emergency. By carrying such a cutter you also may be able to release another pilot who needs help in the event of an accident. (But try the orthodox method of undoing the karabiner first—if you dissect the harness of someone who is only briefly winded, his gratitude is liable to be somewhat muted.)

## Checklist

- Use a stirrup harness.
- Fit an ankle loop, and use a small-diameter stirrup tube.
- Spend plenty of time getting your harness properly adjusted *before* you go out to the hill.
- Dress properly for the job.
- Include your parachute in your pre-flight check routine.

*Dress properly for the job . . .*

Chapter 4
# PREPARING TO SOAR

## Getting used to flying prone

A few years ago it was usual to fly in the seated position. This was inefficient because of the extra drag, and hazardous because of the risk to the spine in the event of a misjudged landing. It also demanded a major adjustment of flying style when the pilot eventually decided to fly prone. Things have changed since then, and you will probably have been taught from the beginning in the 'semi-prone' position, and should not find any difficulty in converting to full-prone.

Before you attempt to fly, be absolutely sure that your glider is rigged with the bar in the correct position for prone flight. On many older gliders the bottom rigging is capable of being adjusted to provide alternative positions for seated or prone: if you are in the slightest doubt about this, get the advice of a really experienced pilot. Similarly if you have a secondhand wing which has been used with a 'trike' microlight, the bar position may not be correct for prone flight.

You should use a stirrup harness with ankle loop as described on page 29, or the fully-enclosed type with the zip removed. Make sure you are hanging about a hand's span above the bar.

Prepare your glider by marking the exact centre of the control bar with a ring of adhesive tape, and prepare yourself by hanging up in the harness somewhere at home, and practising getting in and out of the stirrup lots of times. If you really find the full-prone position unacceptably strange, adjust the harness so that you are still only semi-prone, but don't dispense with the stirrup. Personally I am not too keen on this 'neither one thing nor the other' option, and recommend full-prone from the start.

Your next few flights should be at a site you are already used to—maybe even your original training slope. The first should be arrow-straight, concentrating simply on engaging the stirrup and then getting out of it in good time. You will find out that you really have to push down firmly with your legs to tension the harness, and you must be careful to do this *without* looking anywhere but straight ahead. The other thing to avoid is pushing or pulling on the control bar: all the effort you put into tensioning the harness must be from the hips and legs alone.

The next flight can introduce a couple of turns. Make them quite gentle at first, and avoid letting your legs swing about. Your confidence will grow very quickly, and soon you will be doing 90-degree turns and finding them easier than when there was no stirrup.

Remember to get your undercarriage down in good time for landing. Try to get into the habit of sliding the foot with the stirrup loop off the stirrup first, even at this early stage. This is also the time to develop the habit of grasping the control frame sides as soon as you have rotated out of prone, so that you are in a position to give a really authoritative flare-out on landing.

A lot of beginners make the mistake of thinking that finding the stirrup and going into the prone position must be done at lightning speed. *There is no frantic hurry*—take your time and make your actions positive and accurate. Once you have got the feel of it, repeat the operations a few more times so that you are really comfortable with them.

The marker at the middle of the control frame is to help you keep centralised during longer flights. You probably won't have needed it yet, but it may come in handy next time

*Nicely comfortable in prone, the pilot is weightshifting to initiate a left turn. Note how his body is virtually in line with the keel: avoid the temptation to swing your legs about.*

out, because you are ready to soar properly now!

## Putting all the elements together

You are familiar with your glider and equipment. You can launch, land and make reasonable turns. You know of a good site, so there is absolutely nothing to stop you from soaring except your own confidence ...

### The site

Choose the site which will be the best one for you to learn to soar on, not necessarily the one your more experienced pals just happen to be going to that day. Most important is a smooth take-off area and a safe bottom landing. The bit in between isn't as important as all that, although it needs to be steep enough to develop good lift and give you plenty of ground clearance. Obviously you need something with a generous lift-band, so to a certain extent the bigger the better, although it is understandable if you feel 'psyched out' by a truly awesome site.

There are many hills throughout the British Isles which will do very well. Don't expect them all to be good all the year round, though. Many of the chalk downland sites of the south of England are excellent on a day when the corn has been cut and there is landing space everywhere, but impossible if you are confined to a narrow top landing strip in order to avoid crops. Moorland may be out of bounds at lambing time or during the grouse shooting season, while some coastal sites are closed during the summer holiday period.

These first soaring flights are so important that it is worth driving a lot of extra miles to a really suitable site. Pick somewhere which will allow you to concentrate on flying rather than constantly worrying about the landing.

I will assume you understand that you don't just turn up at another club's site and help yourself to their air. Apart from obvious considerations of good manners and common sense, you will be given much more help if you make prior contact and display a keenness to respect local rules.

### The launch point

Once on the hill, the next decision is exactly where to launch from. I know that sounds fairly obvious—surely you go from where everybody else launches, don't you? You will find out that in spite of all their other sterling qualities, hang-glider pilots as a species are rather lazy. I can think of many sites where the usual launch area is by no means the easiest, but saves a few metres of climbing. As the performance of modern gliders has improved, on certain sites it has even become common to launch from a low spot and then fly across to a main ridge. Very soon the low launch has become the normal one, which is fine for experienced pilots with fifth generation gliders, but useless if you are making your first soaring attempt on a Super Scorpion! Make the necessary investment in time and effort to carry on up to the main ridge and to launch in ideal conditions. Of course, you will have to persuade an experienced pilot to go up there with you to assist, which may be the tricky

*The line of the launch run has had to be carefully chosen at this rugged moorland site. The space clear of rocks is less than a metre wide here.*

part of the operation. A side benefit from the extra climb is that you will find out what the true wind strength and direction is at the top: both can vary considerably compared with a lower point, particularly if there is a pronouced shoulder or gully in between.

Take a good look around before assuming that everybody else knows better!

What you are looking for is a spot where the edge is facing directly into wind, is as smooth and straight as possible, and falls away quite steeply. The straightness means that you will have no trouble with one wing getting out into a faster airstream than the other before launch, and the steepness will get you clear of any ground-induced turbulence with minimum delay. The edge must be rounded to some extent: if it is cliff-like, there will be all sorts of launch and turbulence problems which you should avoid when beginning to learn to soar.

The air coming in over the sea is normally very smooth, which explains the popularity of sites such as Rhossilli for early soaring experience, but bear in mind the importance of a spacious bottom landing: if you have any reservations about the amount of beach available, then go somewhere else. Another consideration is that ideal spots can become full of other novices soaring, which can be rather nerve-wracking.

As usual, the best site guide will

turn out to be an experienced pilot, but when you ask for advice, remember that you are looking for a site on which to learn to soar, which may not be the same as the best soaring site! For example, a hill may be very popular because there is a town or factory right in front which is famous for the thermals it kicks off. That will be fine for the experienced pilots who can handle the rough air and tight landing fields that this may involve, but you should go farther afield to a less challenging ridge.

## The weather

At this early stage in your flying you should depend mainly on more experienced pilots for weather guidance. However you must know the sort of conditions you will require, and also what to avoid! You need *steady* winds in the range of 12–22 mph. These are defined as 'light' and 'moderate' in general weather reports and British Telecom's weather service. The conditions should not be likely to change significantly in the short term,

*Be prepared to carry up to an ideal launch point...*

and there should not be any danger of the lift being so strong that clouds become a threat.

You will find, as a hang-glider pilot, that your life tends to revolve around the weather forecasts. The quality of the public services varies considerably, but if you take the trouble to learn a little about how weather develops, you can gain a reasonable idea of what is going to happen.

The TV services are generally rather pathetic, and it is frustrating to find the armoury of sophisticated satellite equipment being used to give very superficial forecasts, presented by quaint comic characters with curious regional accents. Obeying a habit bred of years, most of us still watch the forecast which follows the mid-evening TV news, although it is presented in an increasingly high-tech style and seems to manage to end up giving less useful information than it did in the days of blackboard and chalk! At the time of writing there are signs that the TV companies are waking up to the demand for better weather presentations, and there

*Waiting for the right wind—patience is an essential virtue for hang-glider pilots!*

seems a fair chance that the standard will improve.

One of the most practical forecasts is not designed for flying at all: this is the late-night Radio 4 forecast for inshore waters. If you are going coastal soaring next day, it is well worth staying up late (about 12.30 am) to catch this broadcast.

On the telephone, AIRMET has replaced the old ATAS service which served well for many years. AIRMET gives quite detailed information: general situation; weather prevailing; warnings; outlook; surface visibility; cloud; freezing level; risk of icing; wind direction and speeds at heights from 1,000 ft to 18,000 ft. Note the way wind comes last—you will find yourself urging the recorded voice to get on with it and get to the bit that really interests hang-glider pilots!

The AIRMET forecast which will probably be of most use to you is the one which covers the 0600–1400hr period, with an outlook up to 2000hr. This is available from about 5.30 am. AIRMET is very expensive to use, so share the info with a group whenever possible.

The accompanying map shows how the country is divided into three areas and fifteen sub-areas, and you will need to have this handy when you make your call.

Another service from the Met Office is *Weathercall*. I don't recommend this; you can easily find that your phone bill has been debited a couple of pounds in return for a very general forecast with a high 'flannel' content.

In your search for weather forecasts, don't overlook the daily papers; several of them print a clear synoptic chart complete with isobars.

Once you have decided where to go, be prepared to be patient if conditions are not quite right for you when you get there. Because of the fickle nature of air, hard-and-fast rules do not work too well, but these generalisations may come in useful:

- The wind is often smoother and more reliable in winter than in summer. Also cold air is more dense than warm air, so it is slightly easier to stay up on light winds in winter. Ridge soaring is a year-round activity.
- At any time of year the wind strength usually drops in late afternoon: in summer it will also get smoother because of declining thermal activity towards evening.
- Sea breezes increase until mid-afternoon. If a coastal site is marginally soarable at 11.00 am, it will probably be much easier by 2.00 pm.
- If the sky looks stormy, expect the air to be rough, even if the windspeed seems reasonable.
- Windspeed increases with height. Don't be surprised if what is a gentle breeze at home has turned into a 25 mph blow at the top of a 2,000 ft hill.
- Cumulo-nimbus clouds are a sign that there is more lift under them than a hang glider can handle. There will also be associated gust-fronts, lightning and danger. When there are cu-nimbs about, the best place for your glider is in its bag.

**AIRMET AREAS**

**TELEPHONE NUMBERS**

**AIRMET FORECASTS**
**(0600 hours to 2300 hours)**

| | |
|---|---|
| **AIRMET SOUTH** | **0898-500 693** |
| **AIRMET NORTH** | **0898-500 692** |
| **AIRMET SCOTTISH** | **0898-500 691** |

## Checklist

- Master flying prone before trying to soar.
- Go to the best possible site.
- Choose the easiest take-off point.
- Learn all you can about the weather.
- Be prepared to wait for the right conditions.
- If you are going soaring on a weekday with a group, call Freefone 2230 to notify low-flying military aircraft of your presence.

*Call Freefone 2230 to notify low-flying military aircraft of your presence . . .*

# Chapter 5
# YOUR FIRST REAL SOARING

## The big day

The big day at last! You have driven a long way to a really suitable site, in the company of a more experienced pilot. Yes, it looks good: wind straight in, and not too strong. Time to start rigging.

Your homework has been quite thorough; you have prepared your glider by tying a red streamer to your kingpost to show that you have yet to complete ten hours in the air, and have been repeating to yourself the rules about breaking right if you find yourself having to avoid another aircraft. You don't think there is anything more you can do except launch and try!

You look at one or two of the other gliders in the air. It doesn't seem too crowded; some of them are quite low while others are several hundred feet up, so there is plenty of separation. You are by now so keen that you almost resent it when your Club Coach suggests that he goes first to check out the conditions. You assist him by acting as wire-man, and note that he swings around a little for the first thirty or forty feet, but after that, apart from occasional slight yawing, the flight looks smooth.

Ten minutes later he is back down again.

'Too rough for you yet' he says. 'There's a lot of thermal activity at this time of the day in summer—better wait until this evening.' Now five or six hours is a long time to wait, especially when your glider is rigged and you have your harness on! You watch many of the regulars launch, fly and land with no apparent difficulty, and by mid-afternoon not only have you convinced yourself that you are well able to handle the conditions, you have also managed to persuade your coach that you can.

When you're right at the edge, clipped in and ready to go, the conditions don't actually feel quite as smooth, but at this stage it's easier to say '*release*' than 'I've changed my mind—I'd rather wait a bit longer'.

*Take your time getting the glider balanced before making your launch.*

You launch quite well, and find yourself hanging on as you climb almost vertically. Not bad, and you found the stirrup without having to think about it! Your first turn was planned to be to the right, but that's when your troubles start: just as you begin the turn, the wing is picked up and turns strongly to the left—it doesn't want to go right at all. All of a sudden your ideas of becoming an instant soaring ace are dashed as what was going to be a smooth right turn entirely in the lift-band suddenly develops into a nightmarish diving turn to the left. Now convinced that the glider is uncontrollable, you heave on the bar and manage to fly away from the hill, down to the bottom, and safety. The whole flight took maybe a minute and a half, during which your mouth went completely dry and every muscle tensed to the maximum. The net result is shattered confidence and a long hard slog back up to the top, even though you don't care if you never fly this site again!

So what went wrong? Lots of people were flying: why weren't they thrown about like you? Why were you singled out to be thrashed about in localised and vicious turbulence? Is hang gliding really always a fight against unpredictable elements once you have left training school?

The answer is very simple. It isn't too rough to fly, it is simply too rough for *you*—yet. All your previous flights have been in conditions monitored by your school instructor, and have been relatively smooth. You have become accustomed to the glider always responding at almost the same speed. As soon as something happens to change this speed of response, you lack the experience to cope with it. On this flight you had the misfortune to get the right wing into the edge of thermal lift which pushed it upwards just as you tried to push it down to turn in that direction. With a bit more experience you will welcome this feeling: you will learn to keep the pressure on, so that the glider goes where you want and you climb up in the extra lift which the thermal gives.

This has been a hard lesson in the ways this unfamiliar new element, the air, behaves when we venture into it. But the lesson has not been a damaging one, and it has reminded you that as soon as you try to force the speed of learning, the air bites back!

By late afternoon the clouds are disappearing from the sky, and the wind has settled down quite a lot. Your coach suggests you have another try. With less confidence this time, you go through your pre-flight routine and eventually make a nice clean launch. However, nerves make you forget which foot goes into the stirrup first, and you soon find that you are some way out from the hill before you dare attempt a turn. When you do, it is almost at the outer edge of the lift band. All that the air here can do is to slow your rate of descent—you need to get closer to the hill to soar properly. The snag is that after your experience in the rougher air earlier, you haven't the confidence to fly in closer: you're afraid of being turned into the hillside which seems to loom above your shoulder. In some respects this is not a bad thing: your first soaring flights must not turn into 'scratching' exercises. Anyway, your brave effort turns into a series of S-turns down to that bottom-landing field again.

If only you had got that first turn in a little earlier ...

There are a lot of 'if onlies' in our sport. Something very similar to this narrative has happened to most of us at the early stages. Let's look at the positive side and see what has been gained from your day:

Firstly, you should have observed that if you can see the pilots in the sky swinging around at all, it is surprisingly rough. From the ground, the movement of a wingtip 200 ft above you which yaws say, 1 metre, appears slight. From the control frame attached to that wing, an unrehearsed movement over the same 1 metre can feel quite spectacular. The large amount of vertical separation was another clue—there has to be more than pure ridge lift to make more than a couple of hundred feet difference on most ridges, and that usually means bumpy thermals are present. (Wave lift is another matter, and beyond the scope of this book.) Then you can console yourself that if the first attempt had taken place in the smoother air of the second, you would almost certainly have stayed above the ridge as planned. And with any luck you will be more prepared to wait a little longer for the right moment next time. Meanwhile perhaps another practice session hanging from the rafters in the garage will ensure that you don't try and put the wrong foot in the stirrup again!

If your luck is exceptional, the weather will be kind the next day, and you will have the opportunity to do it all right without a long delay: however, the nature of weather is such that the more you wish for a fine spell, the more wind and low cloud seem to be inflicted upon you. Spells of bad weather almost uniformly coincide with the delivery of your new glider, which provides for a rare test of patience! The best advice I can give for times such as this is to get some decorating done, because as soon as you've mastered the art of soaring there will be few further opportunities.

When eventually you get back to the hill, you wait until later in the day and manage to soar without any great difficulty. At the beginning of your flight you steadily gain height during the course of the first three beats until you are about a hundred feet above the top of the hill. This is it! Other gliders keep clear of you, and you are able to concentrate on keeping in the best lift. After a few more beats, the idea of top-landing comes into your mind, but the more you look at the landing area, the more difficulty you have in deciding how to approach it. All the time you have been thinking about this, you have been making your turns with just a little less precision, while the wind has also been decreasing slowly but steadily ... It is not long before your hundred feet are down to thirty or forty, and shortly you are struggling to keep above the ridge, let alone top-land! One by one the other gliders slide in and land, leaving you alone and on the way down to the bottom again.

Your coach greets you as he comes

down to give you a hand back up to the top: 'Well done—fourteen minutes! You'll soon be ready to try top-landing at this rate! Did you notice the wind dropping? The smoke from the factory is going almost straight up now. Isn't the view great from above the top—you won't have seen the reservoir at the back before, will you?'

The fourteen minutes is good news—it only felt like five or six. No, you hadn't noticed the wind dropping, and er, should you admit that you still haven't seen the reservoir over the back of the hill? Don't worry, many pilots observe nothing except the edge of the ridge and—essential—other gliders, for the first few flights: the basics of keeping aloft demand their full concentration, and they forget to take in the view at all. Next time you will look at the smoke out in the valley both before and during flight, and soon not only will you have a good look at the water, you'll be counting the windsurfers as well.

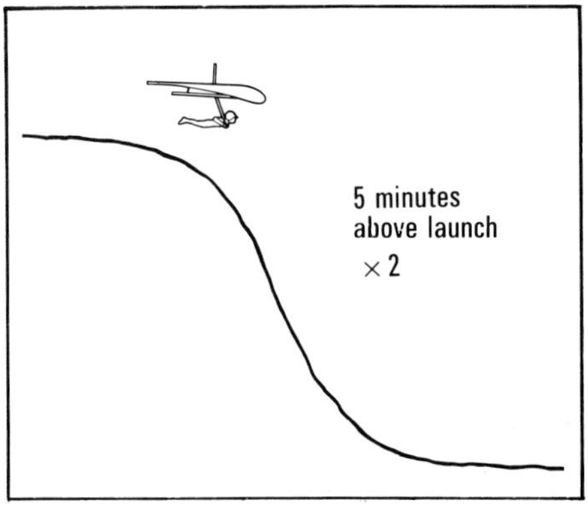


**Fig. 1** *Two soaring flights*

Fourteen minutes is a reasonable flight to enter in your logbook too. You can't stay up that long on sheer luck—you have proved that you are able to fly with reasonable accuracy for sustained periods. Don't dwell on the 'if onlies' now. Yes, it would have been nice to top-land, but you have to admit that you are not skilled enough yet. The main point is that you are a soaring-pilot at last: all you have to do now is to concentrate on becoming a better one.

After a day or two like this, you will have qualified for your P1+, the BHGA's Club Pilot Certificate. In addition to what you have learned in the training school, all it requires are these simple tasks:

- Fly a distance of at least 2 km over a course of not less than 0.5 km between two turn points, and then make a controlled landing within 25 metres of a designated spot.
- Make two soaring flights, each with at least five minutes' duration above take-off. You must use a fourth- or fifth-generation glider.

At some time before your P1+ is signed off, the Club Coach will assess you for attitude and airmanship. You will have to convince him or her that you have developed the attitudes to safety that are essential to *all* pilots, regardless of whether they are flying hang gliders or jets.

Gaining your P1+ also means that you will have qualified for the internationally-recognised *FAI Delta Bronze* badge.

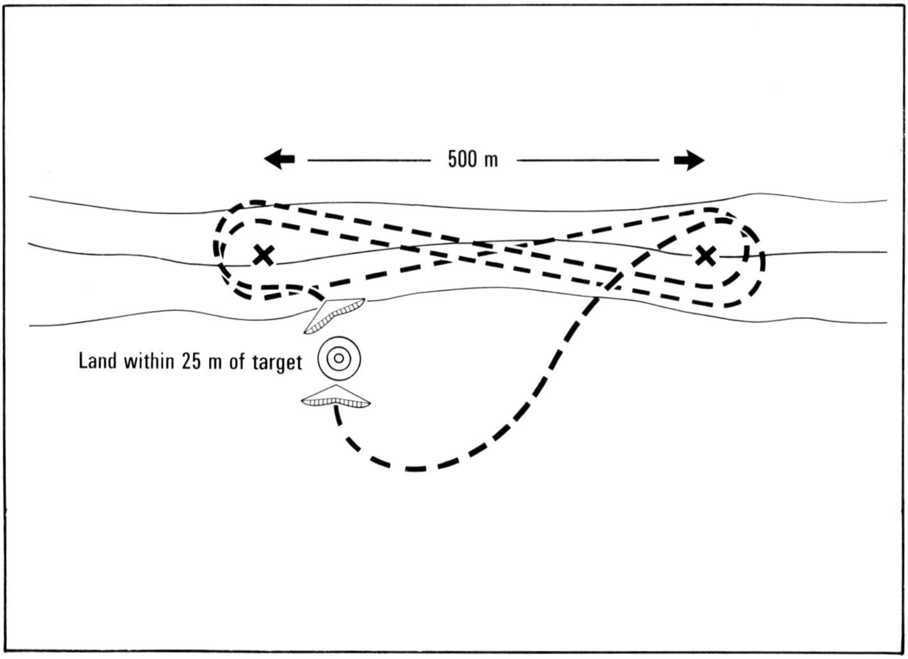


**Fig. 2** *Fly a 2-km course*

Once these tasks have been signed off, you can start to build up the hours which will take you on the way to your next qualification: the *XC Pilot Certificate (P2+)*.

Becoming a cross-country pilot may seem a long way off when you are still mastering the art of ridge soaring, but the time will come in due course. Every minute you gain in the air counts, so be really keen about keeping your logbook up to date.

## The XC pilot's certificate (P2+)

Here are the tasks which you will have to complete for the Cross-Country Pilot's Certificate; you can start to achieve the simpler requirements straight away—don't imagine that they are something to think about in the distant future!

**1** Three launches and landings in a windspeed of *less* than 5 mph (see page 104 for useful tips on this)

**2** Two top landings on each of three sites

**3** Fly five sites (three of them inland ones)

**4** Execute co-ordinated 360-degree turns to left and right

**5** Fly safely, considerately and in accordance with air-traffic rules

**6** Fly a minimum of 30 logged flights after gaining your P1 +

**7** Log a minimum of 25 hours' airtime

**8** Achieve a height gain of 2,000 ft

**9** Make two flights during which ground clearance exceeds 1,000 ft for at least 10 minutes

**10** Attend club lectures on Meteorology, Principles of flight, Air law and navigation, Instrumentation and First aid.

**11** Pass the BHGA theory exam

**12** Undergo a final assessment

You can also qualify for your Delta bronze badge with launches from a tow-line: see Chapter 8.

## Measurements: added confusion!

Units of measurement are curiously combined in aviation. You may have noticed that throughout this book metric measurements are used for most things except height and speed. Although the FAI uses kilometres as units of distance, international air convention still measures altitude in feet, horizontal distances in nautical miles, and speed in knots, while every wind speed meter I have owned has been calibrated in miles per hour, and variometers often read in metres per second!

## Checklist

- Wait until conditions are smooth.
- Respect the judgement of pilots you know to be experienced.
- Learn one thing at a time.
- If you don't understand the 'break right' rule, don't fly!
- Make sure the red or orange ribbon flies from your kingpost: other pilots will give you more space if they know that you are a beginner.
- Try to observe a little more than just the edge of the hill.
- Make it a rule to fill in your logbook every time you fly.

Pennine
Hang Gliding
Centre
Keith Cockroft
Scape View
Golcar
Huddersfield
HD7 4DH
0484 641306
for the best start
in soaring

Chapter 6
# BUILDING YOUR SKILLS

Your first couple of soaring flights will probably turn out to have been pretty mechanical affairs when you look back at them, even if at the time they seemed to be the most exhilarating things you had ever done. However, as your experience grows and your airtime lengthens, you will be able to concentrate on more than just staying in the air.

To progress further you must master the skills of flying on an accurate track, flying at the most effective speed, turning efficiently at different angles of bank, executing 360-degree turns, exploring the outer limits of the lift-band, and being comfortable in the air in the presence of other gliders. We will see how to apply all these skills by flying the 'Shepherd's Hut Run'.

## Flying an accurate track

When ridge soaring, you are inevitably flying cross-wind almost all the time. Consequently if you are to maintain your desired track within the lift-band, your glider must be 'crabbing' along each beat. This means flying straight and level but aiming slightly away from the ridge. It does not mean flying in a constant bank or series of curves. However, many novices fall into the trap of initially compensating for drift by moving across the bar a little to point the nose away from the hill, but then swinging their legs the other way to bring the wing level again. Very soon you find that your body is not in line with the keel: you are flying inefficiently, and the glider feels as if it has a permanent 'turn' built into it. This is where the piece of tape which you fixed around the exact centre of the bar in Chapter 2 comes into its own. It will stop you becoming disoriented relative to the glider, or 'drifting off centre' without realising it.

On that straight ridge where you first soared, you were able to stay in the lift band and out of trouble by simply keeping, say, a wingspan away from the defined edge and maintaining that track. Flying larger, longer ridges with various irregularities demands a little more skill and a lot more imagination, coupled with the ability to maintain an accurate track in places where the edge of the hill no longer provides a completely reliable guide.

## The shepherd's hut run

Let's look at a typical ridge 'somewhere in Yorkshire', and tackle the hazards one by one. The lessons are applicable anywhere!

The experienced pilots talk of the site and ridge as if it is all one smooth entity, and fly from end to end without any apparent difficulty. What they have forgotten is that it really is a collection of soarable features interspersed with one or two very unsoarable ones. You have to learn to clear the unsoarable bits with enough height to sustain on the next soarable part.

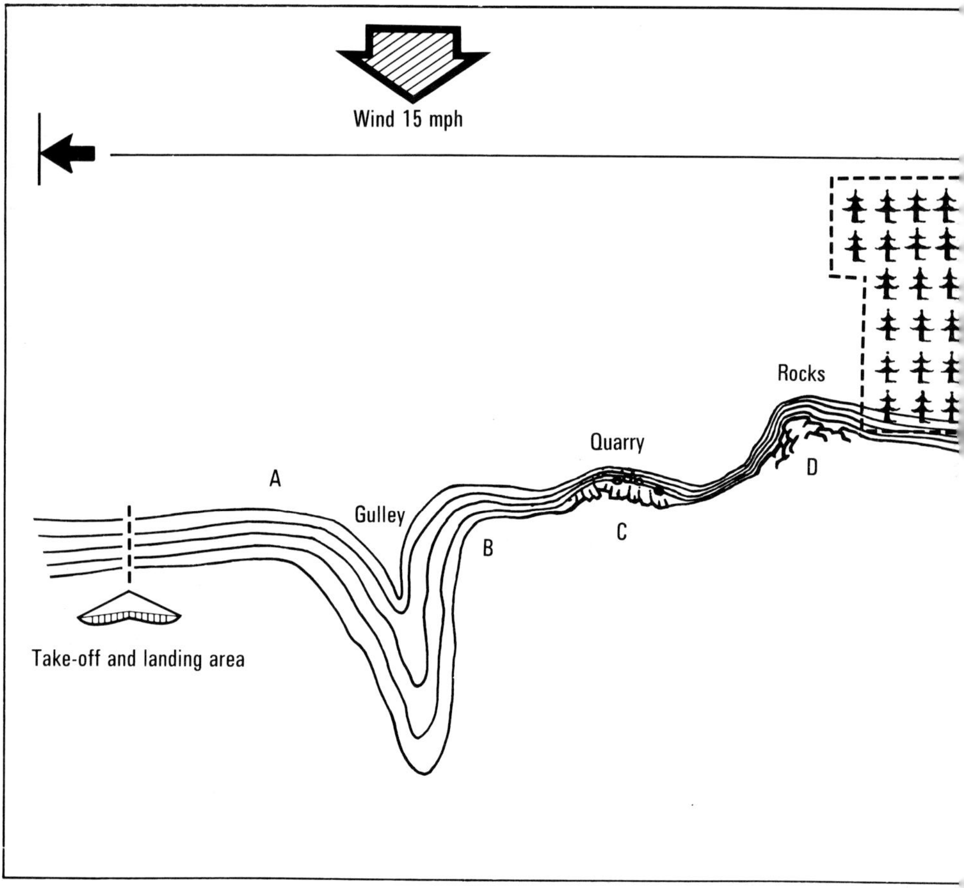

## The gully

If you remember that the trick is to fly across in front of the mouth of the gully, you won't have any trouble here. Fly three or four beats on the take-off ridge, each time easing a little further out from the edge until you are, say, 100 ft above the top, and at point A. It will look quite easy from here, and all you have to do is to pull on speed a little and fly directly to point B. This will be a fast semi-downwind flight, and you should arrive at B comfortably above the top and with some excess speed. You then need to convert your surplus speed into extra height as you soar along towards the quarry. The hazard to avoid, of course, is allowing yourself to get deep into the gully where the only exit is directly into wind but out of lift!

**Fig. 3** *The shepherd's hut run*

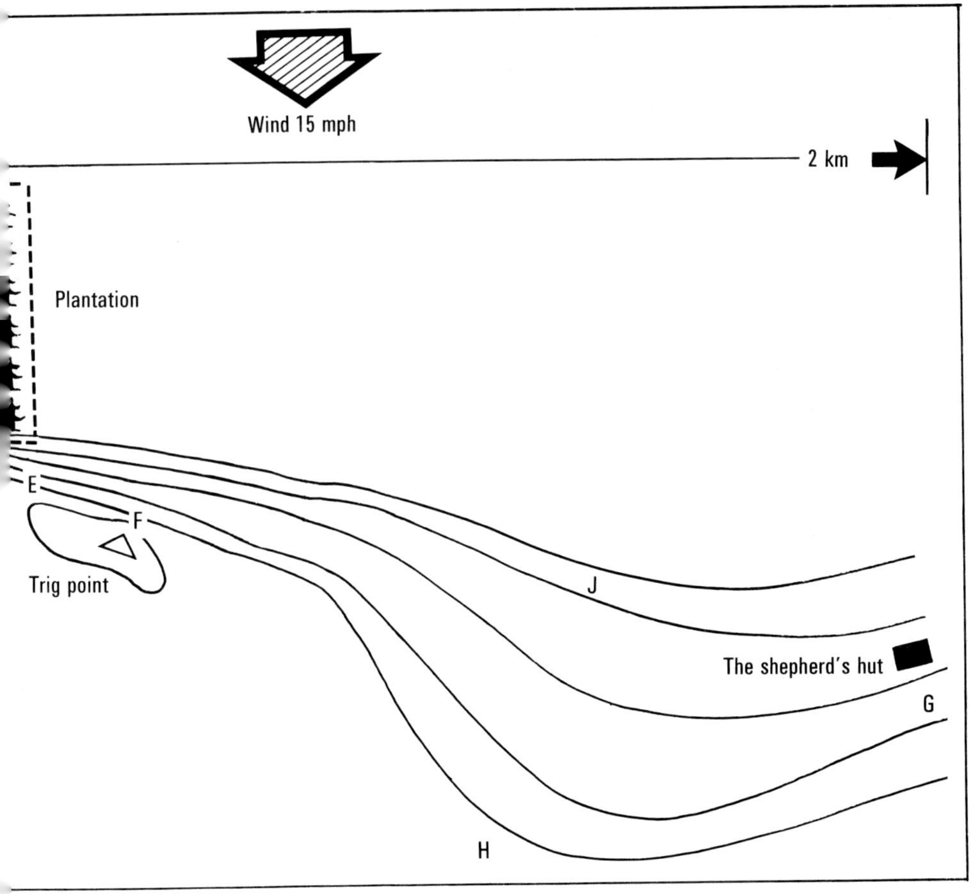

*Just released! The wire-man is given a second to let him get clear: take care if doing this in stronger winds or on cliffs.*

*Lift-off. You can see that the pilot is pulling speed on by the slackness visible in the rear flying wires. His boot has found the stirrup.*

*With both hands on the bottom bar, pressure is finally applied to tension the stirrup.*

### The quarry

There will be no lack of lift at the quarry, which is almost vertical, but if you are low, expect some extra turbulence, and never ever be tempted to try and top-land in the area behind it, at C, because rotors are virtually guaranteed.

### Up to the rocks

The wind will be rather crossed from the right as you fly along to the rocks, so progress will be slower than you may have expected. Don't be tempted to try and hurry the process by flying much faster: you will simply have difficulty maintaining height, and will soon realise that when you arrive at point D you will probably be well below the rocks. If you think that this will happen, fly back to the quarry to gain height for another attempt.

### Behind the plantation

Although there is a reasonable amount of bare moorland above the plantation, take particular care here. If you are not above the top as you pass the rocks at D, you run the risk of sinking-out in the lee of the trees. This will happen with amazing rapidity. When you return, note that the length between the trig point and the rocks is slightly out of wind, so don't let yourself be led into getting too low here. Provided you are definitely above the top of the ridge all the time, you will have no trouble.

### The trig point

The trig point is the highest point on the ridge, and unless you are feeling intrepid, this will be the best place at which to turn before going back to the take-off area. If you are doubtful of having enough height to allow you to pass the plantation safely, fly a number of careful short beats from E to F. Flying short beats like this will sharpen up your turning skills very rapidly. When flying uneven ridges, always be on the lookout for small sub-sections like this which will yield extra height if flown carefully as separate ridges in their own right. The nimble turning ability of a hang glider is a great benefit in places like this! Don't go past F, though, as you will lose all the extra height you gained as soon as you try to get back around the corner!

### Down to the shepherd's hut

You are pushing your luck if, as an inexperienced pilot on an intermediate glider, you decide to carry on down to G. You will reach the hut without any difficulty, but getting back will turn out to be rather challenging. The ridge here has become much shallower while also dropping back quite a long way. When you turn above the hut (thinking 'what an ace I must be to have got this far'), the problems will rapidly become clear. The edge of the hill has disappeared—you seem to be over almost flat moorland, and can't decide exactly the line to fly: if you let yourself go back to H you find that the beat up to the trig point is into wind and yields almost no lift whatever, while if you make your way to J you are well below the level of the top of the plantation, which feels very worrying indeed. In fact, if you keep your head, you will *probably* be able to gain sufficient height between E and F, even though you are close to the ground; but we're not interested in 'probablies' at this stage in your flying. In a few months' time, when you have graduated to a flatter-gliding CFX wing, you will be able to do the 'Shepherd's Hut Run' without any difficulty.

## The speed you need

On that straight ridge where you learned to soar it didn't matter too much how fast you flew, provided you kept safely above stalling speed. Remember the terms:

*Minimum Stalling Speed*: the speed at which the wing suddenly stops developing lift. This is very slow in level flight, but increases rapidly when the glider is banked during turns. Take note—we're talking of *minimum* stalling speed: your glider can be made to stall at *any* speed if you push the bar out too far, too fast. Beware!

*Minimum Sink Speed*: The speed at which your rate of descent is lowest. Only a couple of mph above stalling speed. The best speed to use in the lift band when there's plenty of space around.

*Best Glide Speed*: The speed at which your glide angle is shallowest. Occurs towards the upper end of the speed range. This is the speed to fly across areas of sink.

Of course, you don't simply fly at one speed or the other, but use an infinite variety of intermediate speeds. One of the signs of expert pilots is how little they appear to alter speed: bar movements of an inch or so are enough to give them the desired effects, while the less experienced can be seen rowing themselves around the sky using variations of a foot or more. Practice is the only true way to acquire finesse, but an appreciation of why you need to alter speed helps: so let's take a look at the speed variations along the Shepherd's Hut Run:

## Speed variations

Once clear of take-off, you can slow down to minimum sink speed while you gain enough height to cross the gully. However, you will need to speed up slightly at the end of each beat so that you do not risk stalling in the turns—remember that stall speed increases as you turn, and minimum sink is not far above stall speed to start with. Also, if other gliders are in the sky with you, speed up a little so that directional response is improved when you have to manoeuvre in 'traffic'.

At point A you speed up to best glide speed to cross the mouth of the gully, as far as point B (see page 58). Then it's down to minimum sink as far as the quarry. If it's a bit bumpy in the air over the quarry, speed up just a little so that you can maintain your required track without difficulty, but avoid going flat out: that will only make the bumps feel a lot worse.

Keep the speed close to minimum sink from the quarry to the rocks. Because there is a headwind component on this leg, your groundspeed will be low: don't let this mislead you into speeding up in an attempt to reach the rocks as quickly as you imagine you should. Let the glider take its time, and you will get there with plenty of height to spare.

The stretch above the plantation is easy. The hill goes a little out of wind here, so a flying speed just above minimum sink will take you along to point E quite quickly. If you feel uncomfortably low above the top rows of trees, pull on speed to get past them as rapidly as possible. If you decide to soar the short ridge in front of the trig point between E and F, you will need accurate judgement of speed. The rapid sequence of turns you will require means that you must fly faster than you would otherwise think necessary. Because you will be above minimum sink, it will take more beats to make height than you may have imagined.

If you were over-bold and decided to make for the shepherd's hut, you should have flown there at somewhere around best glide speed. Bearing in mind the overall tailwind component on this leg, the hut will have been reached easily and fast. Coaxing the glider back again is the tricky bit. If there is enough lift between the hut and J to sustain your glider, then fly at minimum sink speed. If you are sinking at all, however, you want to be out of the sinking air as quickly as possible. Keep an eye on the top of the plantation and try to judge whether you are rising or falling relative to it—at this point the hill itself won't be a very good guide, and the fact that you are below the top at all will make you feel *very* low! If you are rising, then fine—keep flying as slowly as safety allows: if you are still going down, speed up towards maximum glide speed until you are well past point J where the ridge begins to steepen again. There you have a chance, and provided you fly economically you should be able to regain all your lost height in a few beats in front of E to F. The feeling of relief as the trig point comes back into view will be enormous!

*Safety special*: if you are 'pushing your luck' in a spot like this, remember to fly a little faster when you get near the hill—don't get caught out by the wind gradient. And if you have any real doubts about your ability, fly *out and down* to safety. The worst decision you could make would be to 'hope for the best' and end up being dumped by the rotor behind the plantation corner near E.

## Checklist

- Look ahead and try to fly smooth tracks.
- Keep your body in line with the keel when flying each beat.
- Think about flying speed, and don't try to 'force' progress over the ground.
- Choose the right speed for each part of your flying site.
- When flying a long ridge, always keep the return journey in mind.

Chapter 7

# TURNS, TOP LANDING AND THE LIFT BAND

## Turns

### Co-ordinated turns

The more time you spend on the ridge, the greater will be your opportunities for polishing up your turning technique. On a flight such as the Shepherd's Hut Run, you will start off by doing a few quite gentle turns, each of a little more than 180 degrees, at each end of the beat as you gain height on the first part of the ridge. Then you will use a very small degree of bank as you turn parallel with the ridge again at B. Between B and D the lift will be very good; somewhere like this provides ample opportunity to practise much tighter turns, which are performed by speeding up the glider, then making a very positive sideways move on the bar of say 20–25 cm before easing it out and progressively allowing yourself to move back to the centre at the apex of the turn. Then you pull on a little as you shift slightly towards the other corner of the bar in order to straighten the glider up again.

At first you will find that your turns go either just a little too far, or not quite far enough, but constant practice will soon teach you to bring the glider out of a steep turn with the nose pointing exactly in the direction you wish, and at the correct flying speed.

Once you can co-ordinate well in this way, you are ready to do 360-degree turns. These are only two 180's joined together, and provided you start off with a good reserve of height, there is no mystery about them. The main thing to watch is that you do not become disoriented—make sure you know where the ridge is all the time.

360's are not of any particular value purely for ridge soaring, but mastering them is a skill best learned while on the ridge, and also a great confidence-builder.

Whatever sort of turn you are practising, from gentle yaws up to quite steeply banked 360's, be certain at all times that you are well clear of

*Into a tight 360. You should try to keep your body better aligned than this.*

other gliders and have a good surplus of height.

Even if you have a lot of height to spare, do not be tempted to perform multiple 360's at this early stage—it is very easy not only to build up speed into a fast spiral dive, but also to lose all sense of where you are!

## Flat turns

Some pilots, on some gliders, seem to display the ability to perform perfectly flat turns. Beware of trying to copy them: this is a tricky art to master, and because each glider responds differently to attempts to yaw it, much of the learning must come from experiment. It is not a technique for use in normal ridge soaring at all, and should only be added to your armoury of skills for use when really high in light thermals. However, if you want to know how it is done, here is the method ...

As you have found out, when you turn a glider using weight-shift in the normal way, the angle of bank increases and speed has to be increased accordingly: obviously your sink rate suffers in the process. But if you use the *inertia* of your body around which to pivot the glider, you can change direction with virtually no roll at all.

The method involves breaking the rule you have been taught always to keep your body in line with the keel. For example, to turn left, first swing your feet and trunk some way across to the right, keeping your left arm virtually fixed and collapsing the right elbow. After a very slight delay, the glider will start to do a badly co-ordinated turn to the right, but before this has fully developed, swing to the left in a smooth and positive manner by straightening the right elbow and collapsing the left one. Overall there should be no fore-to-aft weight-shift, just a swivelling of the body. The glider should now perform a flat yawing turn to the left which can be easily stopped by returning to the parallel position in the centre of the bar.

The general effect should have been of a slight feint to the right followed by a smooth turn to the left. If you had simply swivelled left without the initial move to the right, the result would probably have been the start of a rather inefficient diving left turn.

The more stable the glider, the more difficult it will be to make it yaw-turn. On some trainers you will be completely wasting your time!

**Note** Because this manoeuvre is performed close to the stall, it must *only* be practised at a good height, in lifting air well above the ridge. It is no substitute for normal, banked and co-ordinated turns for all utility flying. It is *never* for use when 'scratching' for lift close to the ground.

## Adverse yaw

While attempting slow, gentle turns, you may find that initially your glider seems to go in exactly the *opposite* direction to the way you have weight-shifted. Not quite what you expected, surely—weren't you always taught 'move right to go right' and so on? The answer is that you have uncovered the mystery of adverse yaw, which is responsible for this effect. In crude terms, what happens is this: as you move over, the small amount of weight-shift you apply loads that wing more than the other, and when you add weight to a wing, it speeds up. So at the beginning of the turn you have a situation where the precise opposite of what you desire is happening: the wing you move to is trying to fly around the other one!

This effect usually shows up when attempting gentle turns at low speed, and it only lasts for a short time just as the turn is initiated: very soon the glider overcomes the adverse yaw and the turn continues normally.

Although they look so simple, our flexible wings involve a complex range of aerodynamic effects, some of which exaggerate the adverse-yaw tendency, while others tend to cancel it out. In my experience adverse yaw is more noticeable on gliders with relatively stiff airframes.

## Handling crosswinds on a ridge

One of the facts of life is that the wind is rarely blowing absolutely straight at the hill: usually it is at least a few degrees off to one side or the other. This gives rise to a number of effects, none of which need necessarily spoil your day, provided you make the appropriate allowances. The amount of crosswind which still permits you to fly will vary according to the site and the wind strength. As a newcomer to soaring, you should look upon 15 degrees as the top limit, although on some sites the experts will still manage to stay up when it is crossed by 30 degrees or more.

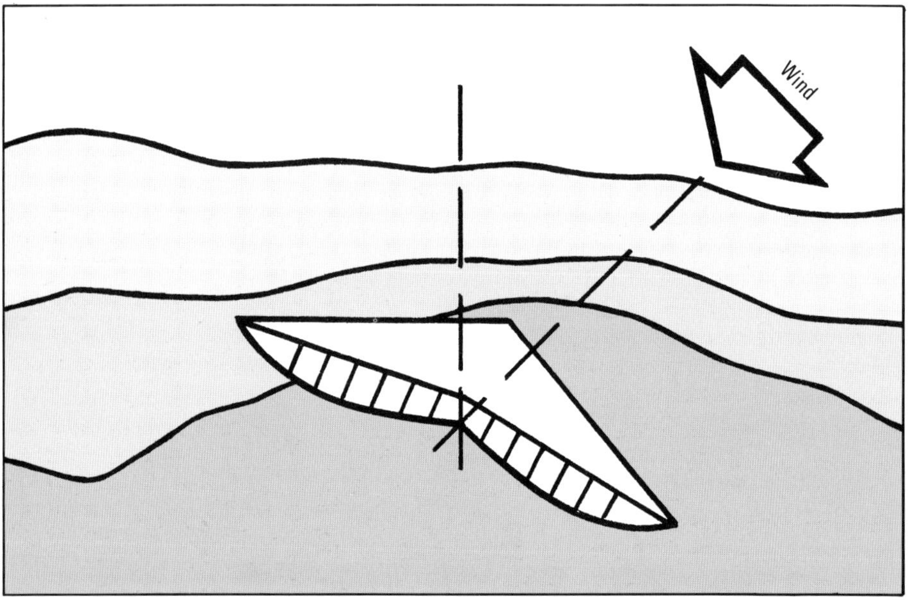

If you remember the following points, you should avoid any nasty surprises:

**1** If the wind is crossed on the edge of a hill, it will almost certainly be very much more crossed at the bottom of it. Expect to have to land virtually parallel with the ridge if you fly down. The steeper the hill, the more pronounced this effect will be.

**2** Pick your launch site with care. If you walk a few yards, you can often find somewhere on a ridge which is slightly less out of wind than the rest.

**3** Line up with the glider pointing into the wind, rather than straight out from the hill, *but* be certain that you don't let one wing get too far out into the airstream while the other is still in wind-shadow behind the edge. Bob Harrison, the BHGA's training officer, suggests a simple rule to minimise the crosswind effect: launch towards a point which is halfway between the direction of the wind and a line straight out from the hill.

**Fig. 4**
*Launch towards a point which is halfway between the direction of the wind and a line straight out from the hill. Take care not to get one wingtip picked up by the airstream.*

**4** Make your attack of the take-off run even more positive and determined than usual.

**5** Make your first beat *into* wind: that will mean that you are moving over the ground quite slowly, and so will stay in the lift for the longest possible time on the first beat. Don't let your apparent low speed tempt you into pulling the bar in too far. Fly at your normal cruise speed, and take your time.

**6** Expect the downwind beat which comes next to be quite a contrast! You will seem to be racing down the ridge. This time you must be careful to keep your speed high enough—you may feel that you want to slow down so that the groundspeed feels more normal: *don't do it*. Prepare for the next turn in good time so that you don't find yourself being carried further than you intended.

**7** Make the most of any irregularities which are less out of wind; they can often yield good lift.

**8** If you are planning to top-land, make your approach during the beat into wind.

**9** Be aware of your limitations. On a normal hill site, if the wind is blowing more than 20 mph, and is approaching 15 degrees off, save flying until another day. Really steep cliffs are less tolerant than that, so be extra cautious.

## Top landing

Once you have developed the skill of landing back on top of the hill after most flights, you will find that your rate of learning increases considerably. Being able to keep your flights to a length which prevents you becoming tired, and then taking off again with a minimum of preparation, is a great advantage which tow- and mountain-launched beginners do not share, so you should cultivate the art of top landing as soon as you safely can.

It is really very easy: all you have to do is to fly your glider back beyond the lift band and into horizontal wind, where it will descend at its normal sink-rate. Provided that it is pointing into wind throughout the descent, and that the air through which you pass is smooth, you will land gently. Because it is easy, don't imagine that it is without its hazards—you must work at avoiding them. Breaking the operation down into three distinct phases will make it simpler:

Phase one is the *planning* stage, when you choose a part of the ridge where the flow will be smooth, both where you fly back over the edge, and also directly in front of where you are going to land. This is when you decide where you will land, and from which direction. Apart from the smoothness of the hill, you need to be sure that there are no obstructions —buildings, trees etc.—which could disturb the airflow. Also check that the way is clear in case you find you need to overshoot and fly out again; don't come in directly behind parked gliders. If the wind is not completely square-on, make your approach from the more downwind direction.

Phase two covers *approach and positioning*. In a moderately strong wind, the whole process will be quite easy, and you will be able to 'crab' across the top of the site, with the nose of your glider almost directly into wind all the time. Assuming that you have gone sufficiently far back in the first place, you will find yourself descending almost vertically with a minimum of drama.

The actual *descent and landing* form phase three. The key to a safe descent is simply to keep a reasonable amount of airspeed on so that you do not get caught out by the wind gradient effect, while all the time pointing *directly into wind*. As soon as you touch down, get the control bar onto the ground, and step through the frame to take hold of the front wires so that there is no danger of the nose of the glider being picked up by the wind.

*A beginner brings his Atlas in for a top landing. His confidence is helped by the presence of someone who will take the nose-wires as soon as he touches down.*

The height from which you should attempt a top landing will vary according to the site and your increasing skill, but in the early stages of soaring, a hundred feet clear of the top should be considered the absolute minimum. That will ensure that you have enough height to fly well back, and still have time to concentrate on keeping the nose of your glider precisely into wind throughout the descent.

The commonest error made by novices is not to go far enough back to land. This is the reason for repeated overshooting. When the wind is just strong enough for soaring, overshooting can be a real problem. It is often because the novice is trying to make the classic 'crabbing' approach which appears in all the books (my own included!) in conditions which are too light to allow it. Try this modified approach when soaring lighter winds: cross the edge at a shallow angle, and, keeping some speed in hand, fly along the top of the ridge almost parallel to it, but quite well back. You will steadily lose height, so when down to about forty or fifty feet, turn smoothly into wind and land in the normal manner. Of course this approach will only work on a long ridge, and should not be attempted if you are not confident of being able to judge the height and to execute the turn properly. However, because the whole manoeuvre and landing is carried out at normal flying speed, it is potentially safer than trying to make an excessively slow 'crabbing' approach in lightish winds.

Whatever happens, if you think there is a chance that you will run out of hilltop before you have concluded your landing, make the decision to fly out again in good time: return to prone position and pull on some speed to fly out over the edge again. Avoid the danger of trying to do a panic stop, and finishing up stalled-out as you tumble over the lip.

Some hills or ridges have a wall or fence running along the top, and sometimes this can make a good guide to the track to fly when lining up for a top landing.

If you are following the advice to go well back, beware of the sort of hill which drops away again behind the normal landing area. The wind shadow in such places can be very severe, and you must be prepared to keep plenty of speed on during the final part of the descent, and to be ready for a fast running landing if need be.

Safety note: Top landings inevitably involve making turns close to the ground. You will be passing through wind gradients and shear levels. Never let yourself become casual about the operation: concentrate on getting it right every time. It is unfortunately true that the highest proportion of reported accidents are the result of poorly executed top-landings.

## Exploring the lift band

The lift band is not a permanent feature with defined edges: being constructed from moving air it naturally alters with every change of wind speed and direction. As your flying confidence increases, you will be able to fly to its outer limits, secure in the knowledge that at any time you can turn back towards the hill to find lift again.

Your first visits to these outer limits will probably occur when soaring a small ridge with a few other gliders present. Sooner or later you will have to move right a little to make space for a glider coming towards you (remember? *break right!*) and may easily find yourself going down because you have gone too far out from the hill. This happens if you stray out to the point where the air you are flying through is no longer going upwards faster than you are sinking.

The upper limit can be found by flying really economically at minimum-sink speed, easing the bar out a centimetre at a time as you creep up and out above the edge of the hill. By patiently easing the glider along above promising-looking spots, and at varying distances from the front, you will eventually reach a height where your sink rate is balanced by the available lift, and no matter how carefully you fly there is no more altitude to be gained. Needless to say, you don't attempt this really slow style of flight until you are safely clear of the ground: remember, minimum-sink speed is uncomfortably close to minimum stalling speed! At the top of the lift band, the wind will be stronger because of wind-gradient, and will also be travelling horizontally as far as you are concerned. Don't become so intent to gain the last few feet of height that you allow yourself to be blown back behind the ridge.

The rearward limit of the lift band is obviously to be found behind the edge of the hill. It is usually quite clearly defined, and flying behind it is necessary in order to top-land. The steeper the hill, the more pronounced the back edge of the lift band: the extreme case is a cliff, where not only does the band stop abruptly, but an area of lethal sink or rotor may lie immediately behind it.

## Checklist

- Practise turns both to left and right.
- Practise both steep and shallow turns.
- Understand the three phases of a top landing: decision, position and descent.
- Land well back from the edge.
- If you think you may overshoot, make the decision to fly out again in good time.
- Watch out for wind gradient and wind shadow.
- Explore the limits of the lift band once you have mastered the basics of just staying within it.

# Chapter 8
# OUT OF RIDGE LIFT

## Making the most of tow-launches

All the theory and good intentions in the world are no substitute for hours in the air when it comes to perfecting the art of flying hang gliders. Every flight adds something to your skills in a way that cannot be matched. As ridge soaring is the simplest way of accumulating airtime, this book naturally spends a lot of space on it. However, that is not much consolation if you happen to live far distant from ridges that lie obligingly across-wind. Fortunately modern towing techniques now provide an alternative way for lowland fliers to gain height, and here we look at ways of getting the most from that height.

If you learn to fly from a towline initially, you are likely to encounter the 360-degree turn at an early stage: in fact it will be probably be the first thing you learn after your most basic training. Hill-trained fliers may be surprised at this, but it is simple when you think about it: you take off at the downwind end of a field, and release

*An instructor tries out an Atlas on the towline. Note how he is using a stirrup elastic which goes around the foot rather than the ankle. This method works well, but I still have a preference for the method described in Chapter 3—the stirrup is then more out of the way when running.*

toward the upwind end; the usual flight pattern is then to turn and fly downwind for the length of the field before making a further turn into wind prior to landing close to your starting point. That all adds up to a 360, even if it is called a 'circuit' and is very large indeed! Of course, the step from flying big open circuits to turning 360's which are tight enough to keep you within the boundaries of an area of thermal lift is one which will take a little time to learn. Finding the thermals is another matter too!

Choosing the best speed at which to fly is probably the most difficult skill to acquire. In stable conditions you need to be moving at minimum-sink speed to make the most of your time in the air, but as soon as you start to turn, that speed will be too close to the stall for comfort. As usual the answer is a compromise, and involves very smooth, steady changes of speed. A few centimetres of bar movement are the most that are needed at any one time. But for safety's sake, err on the side of extra speed if in any doubt at all. When you begin to work any lift, you find that flying speed becomes more critical.

Here is a suggested schedule for progressively improving your soaring performance from a tow-launch: you must only attempt to fly these patterns with the full knowledge of the chief flying instructor and winch crew at your site. In many places there may be local rules which require you to turn in a specific direction immediately after launch, and such rules *must* be obeyed.

In these examples it is assumed that you are being launched directly into wind and are free to fly anywhere over the field. Take particular care that none of the exercises takes your flight path over the active winch-line or runway.

## 1 Accurate circuits

Try to fly the circuit with defined turns at the corners, getting the wings level as you fly the legs between turns. What you are aiming at is shown in Fig. 5, but because of the drift induced by the wind, you will probably end up with something like Fig. 6.

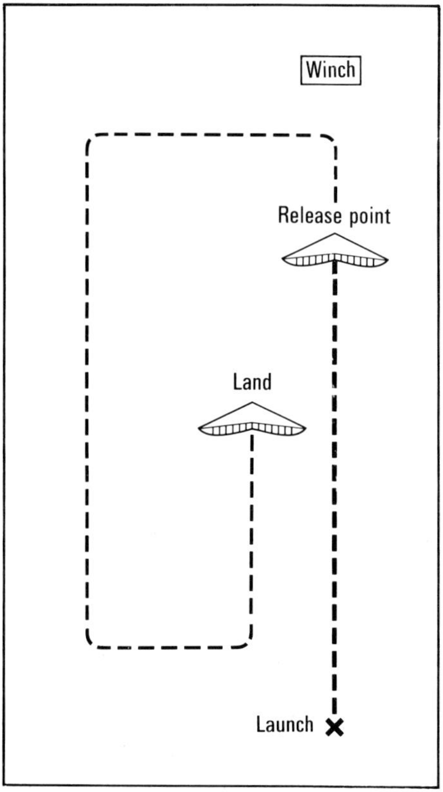


**Fig. 5** *A simple circuit in still air*

After you have made several flights over both left- and right-handed circuits, you should be getting familiar with the height required to leave a comfortable margin when making your final turn into wind prior to landing. You will also have begun to learn just how rapidly your glider covers the ground when flying downwind, yet how steeply it descends as soon as you try to make it penetrate back into wind. These are some of the essential skills which the hang glider pilot must acquire; they must become instinctive, and the most expensive set of instruments in the world is no substitute for basic airmanship learned a step at a time.

## 2 Stretching the circuit

The next step is to extend your circuit by incorporating an S-turn at the start of the downwind leg: simply continue your second turn through more than 90 degrees, and follow it with a turn in the opposite direction to take you down to your usual third turning point.

As your total of launches mounts up, so will your skill in getting height

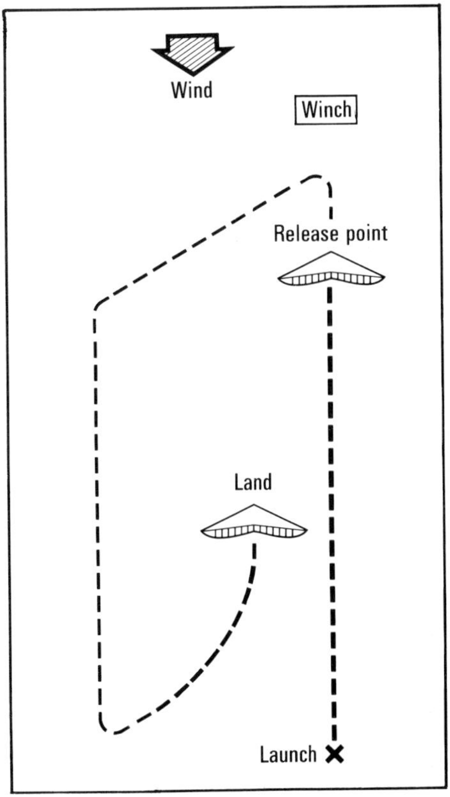


**Fig. 6** *A simple circuit allowing for wind*

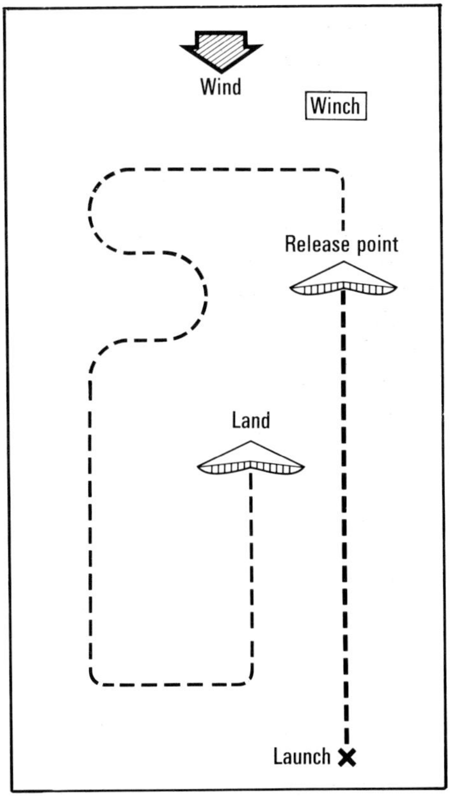


**Fig. 7** *Add an S-turn to your circuits*

at the release point. Before long you will be able to include a series of S-turns into your pattern. Try to fly a similar number of left- and right-hand circuits until you can turn smoothly in either direction. Most pilots have a preference for turning one particular way, and whereas ridge soarers *have* to make alternate direction turns whether they like it or not, the tow-launched flier can get away with almost always going around in the preferred direction unless a positive effort is made to introduce variety!

The ability to turn in either direction with equal ease will prove to be quite an asset when you begin to try to stay in thermals. Skill at S-turning is almost as useful as the ability to perform neat 360's in some conditions. It can be much safer to S-turn to get established in a good thermal if you are not sure exactly where other gliders may be, or how close they are.

## 3 The first true 360's

After the S-turns these will be no trouble at all: at the second turnpoint in your circuit simply pull on a little more speed than usual, bank the glider firmly but not too steeply—about 15 or 20 degrees for

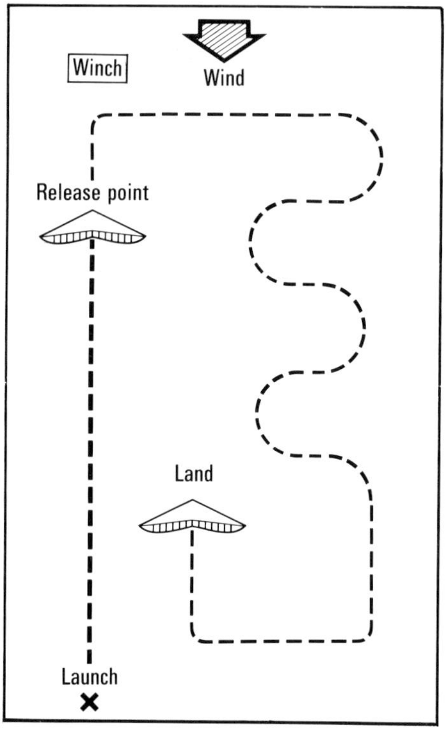


**Fig. 8** *Practise turns to both left and right*

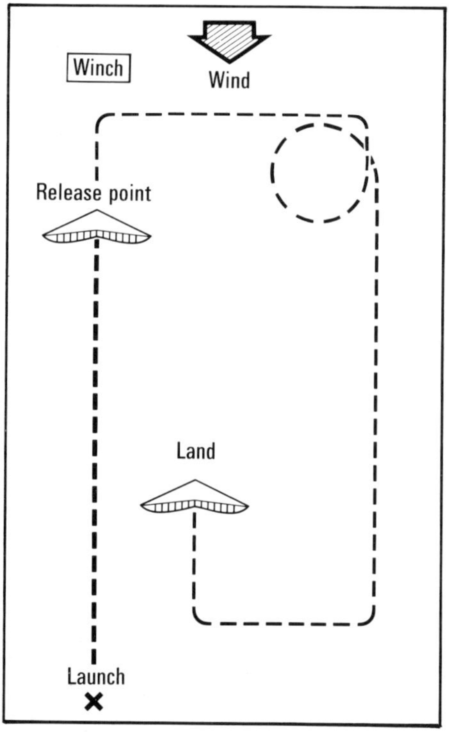


**Fig. 9** *Develop the art of the 360-degree turn*

these first 360's—and push out to start the wing turning properly. Then steadily move back to the centre of the bar without pulling-on, and the turn will continue smoothly. Just as with ridge soaring, you will have to try to stop the turn a little before the nose of the glider is pointing in the direction you want to go, as there is inevitably a slight control delay. Your S-turning experience will come in useful here, as leaving a 360 is a very similar procedure to reversing direction in an S.

360's are easy, but don't try them unless you are confident that there is a surplus of height. Sooner or later you will perform a badly-coordinated one and discover just what an appetite for altitude they can have. Keep a keen look-out for other gliders, and don't turn unless the sky is definitely clear. Fortunately one of the advantages we hang-glider pilots enjoy over any other type of aircraft is that we have completely unrestricted downward vision. There is no excuse for not being aware of other gliders being launched from your field.

Make sure that you do not become so entranced by your skill and expertise when doing these first 360's that you allow yourself to drift downwind beyond the limits of the field.

So far all your tow-launches should have been made in fairly smooth air, but as your glider handling skill increases you will be sent off into conditions where you will begin to encounter thermal lift. If you are still at the 'iron-grip-on-the-bar-and-sometimes-paralysed-with-fear' stage, you should continue to keep to the stable conditions of early morning and evening. If you are able to fly while fairly relaxed, and the glider consistently goes where you want it to, then you can start to seek out thermals and exploit their energy. To do this you will need a basic *variometer*. Normally called simply a 'vario', this instrument tells you whether you are going up or down at any given time, and at what rate.

I don't think it is a good idea for ridge-soaring pilots to start using instruments at a very early stage in their careers; it simply presents an unnecessary distraction. However, if you are being tow-launched there is a much better case for it. If you don't try to work lift once you have become used to the launch process, your flying simply won't ever progress beyond the circuit stage. You will end up with lots of flights but low overall airtime.

## Variometers for beginners

Varios can come with a bewildering variety of specifications. They can indicate lift or sink by means of a visual scale, by sound signals, or by a combination of both. Some will offer a range of options so that you can alter the sensitivity, select the best speed at which to fly, switch to spare batteries, or even ignore climb and sink induced by changes in flying speed. To start with, all these options will only confuse you and may actually slow down your learning rate, so you do not have to spend a fortune on your first variometer. All you need is a reliable instrument without a vast range of extras. It should have a visual read-out, but the most important features are a clear audible tone and the ability to return to zero accurately every time. If the tone sounds on 'up' only, then so much the better for a beginner, as you won't even have to work out which tone means what! (Many models have a switch which allows you a choice of 'up only' or 'up and down' for the tone, and that *is* an option worth having.)

If you are buying secondhand, try to find out if the company which made the model you are considering is still in business: many firms have come and gone, and repair of a defunct model can be difficult or impossible.

## Theory and practice at the landing field

The pilot who learns to soar above a ridge can get away with a fairly sketchy notion of how much ground the glider will cover depending on whether it is flying either against, or with, the wind. (The difference is colossal!) In fact ridge-soarers will go to considerable lengths to avoid flying fully downwind for any length of time. The tow- or mountain-launched pilot cannot afford the luxury of such ignorance, and soon has to develop a working knowledge of the effect which the wind has on the glide angle relative to the ground. As you become increasingly proficient at launching, the speed of the winds in which you can fly also increases, so this topic becomes much more important. Let's look at some examples.

To keep the sums simple, we will assume that the glider has a glide ratio of 8:1 at an airspeed of 20 mph, and that at the same speed its sink-rate is 200 feet per minute.

*Still air*: From 200 feet the glider covers 1600 ft, and takes one minute to do it.

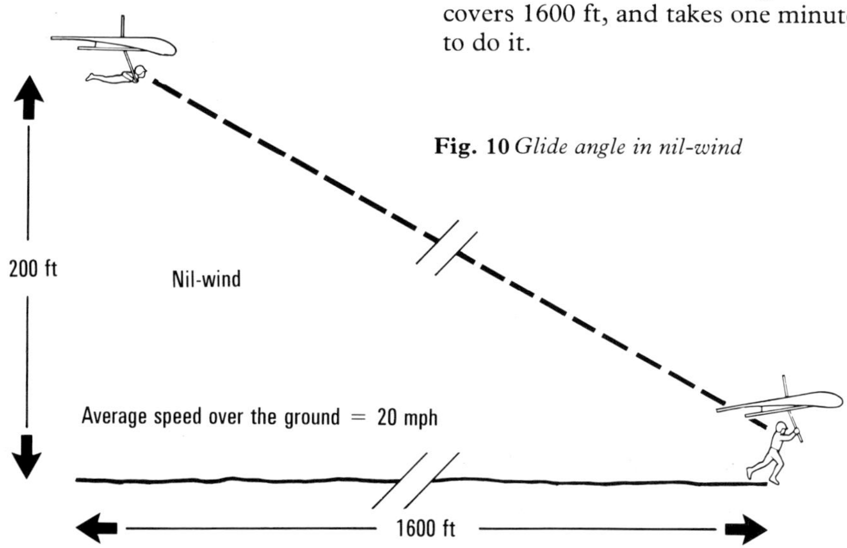


**Fig. 10** *Glide angle in nil-wind*

*20 mph headwind*: The glider descends vertically, making no headway at all, but still takes exactly a minute to reach the ground.

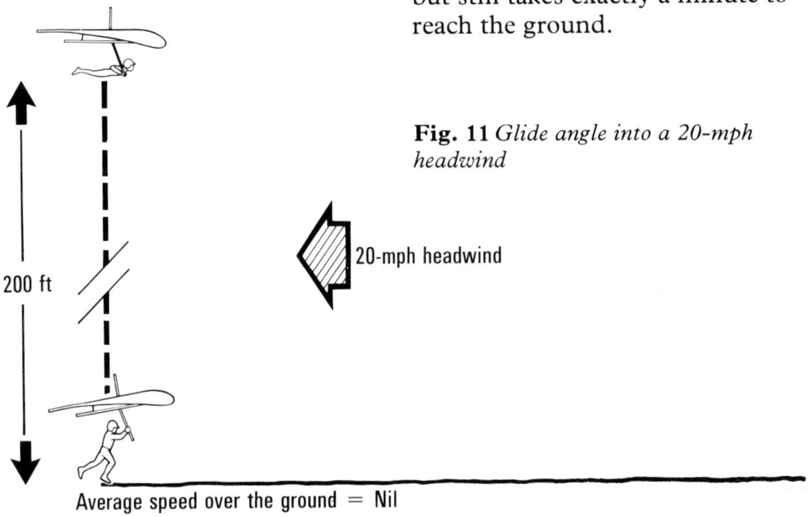


**Fig. 11** *Glide angle into a 20-mph headwind*

*20 mph tailwind*: The other extreme. Although passing through the air at the same speed as in the previous examples, the glider covers 3,200 feet (two-thirds of a mile) over the ground in a minute, and the effective glide ratio has become 16:1.

**Fig. 12** *Glide angle with a 20-mph tailwind*

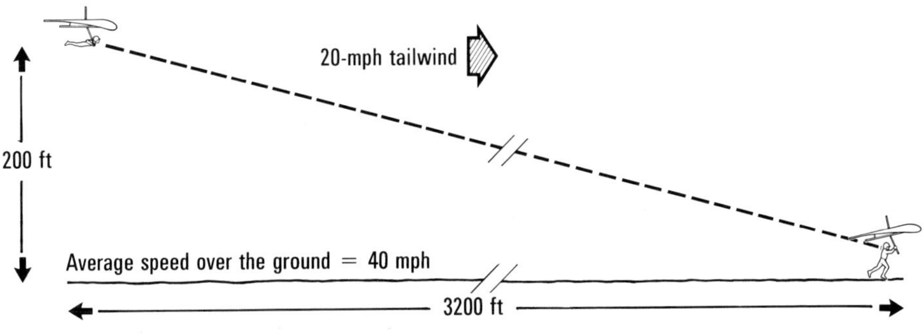

These examples are very simple, and ignore such details as wind gradient and the need to keep some height in hand for the turn into wind prior to landing. But they do illustrate the huge difference the wind makes, and how important it is not to let yourself get taken too far downwind.

When you begin to experiment with your newly-acquired variometer, you must not let yourself become so hypnotised by its messages that you drift too far away from the field.

Now that you own a vario, and have the confidence to fly your glider in slightly bumpy air, just how do you go about using it to add minutes to your flight times? There are many parts to the answer, but as with all the other elements involved in mastering the art of hang gliding, it is the methodical approach which will bring results most quickly. Of course, a little luck is also going to help!

## Finding thermals

You will know that what you are seeking are columns or bubbles of rising warm air called *thermals*. They usually originate from uneven heating of the ground, and come in a vast variety of shapes and strengths, but all suffer from the severe drawback of being invisible. They can be from a few metres in diameter to what can feel like a kilometre or so. A strong thermal is quite capable of making you climb at a thousand feet per minute, while a weak one may simply allow you to sustain your height for an additional minute or two. The vario will help you to 'see' the thermals, by telling you when you fly into their lift, but you must assist the process by positioning your glider where you are likely to find one. Once in the lift, the vario will help you to turn or circle so that you stay within it.

The longer you are in the air, the more likely you are to find a thermal, so work on your towline technique to get the best release height you can.

Thermals travel downwind, and, within very broad limits, may be considered to move at the speed of the wind. Therefore you stand the best chance of staying in one if you have the length of the field downwind of you when you enter it.

Because dark ground absorbs radiant heat from the sun more rapidly than the rest, dark areas like car parks and ploughed fields are frequently thermal generators: if there is a choice, you will find that you will usually do better if you can position yourself directly downwind of such an area.

Imagine that you are being towed up at about three o'clock on a spring afternoon. The wind is only about 8 mph, but you have a bumpier ride than any of your previous launches. Turning left after release, you track crosswind to the corner of the field. Instead of stringing together the succession of 360's which you had previously been experimenting with, you make a 180-degree turn back towards your release point. The vario remains quiet until you turn towards the corner of the field again: just as you fly past the car-park, the nose of the glider is tugged upwards, and the vario begins to squeak. You are in a thermal! Every second you can stay there will yield a height-bonus and stretch your airtime. The ideal reaction is for you to count to three and, if the vario is still singing, start to turn neat 360's completely within the thermal.

Usually in the first few thermal encounters you find yourself being spat out of them just as soon as you find them, and discover for yourself that all that lift is surrounded by lots of sink ... Also there is no guarantee that you will fly straight into a thermal; as often as not they will make their presence felt by pushing one wing up, which can be rather disconcerting for a beginner.

Even before you have learned how to plot out the size and shape of thermals with any accuracy, you can extend any flight quite simply when there is lift about. All you need to do is remember the rule:

- Slow down in lift; speed up in sink.

If you are flying your circuits at a little above minimum sink speed as usual, your vario will probably be reading a fairly constant 200 feet per minute rate of descent. If this suddenly increases to, say, 300 feet per minute, pull some speed on immediately, as you want to be out of this sinking air as rapidly as possible. After a short time you may be lucky enough to encounter the thermal on the other side of the sink. When you do, you should reduce speed to as close to the minimum sink rate as you can judge. Bear in mind that if your vario says you are sinking at 100 feet per minute, you are still extending your flight and gaining from the thermal lift. Any reading of less than 200 feet per minute is a bonus!

If you stick to this simple rule you will certainly stay aloft for longer than if you fly at a constant speed.

Learning to work thermals is a slow and often frustrating business, but if you are persistent you are bound to find them. Watch out when you do begin to stay with them that you don't concentrate on looking at the needle of the vario so much that you become disoriented. It is really easy to forget to to keep a lookout for the towline or other gliders at this time. It is also easy to let yourself travel out of range of the field, and you need more experience before going off cross-country!

Fig. 15 would be a reasonable flight pattern to aim for if you are really serious about finding thermals. The chances of finding one that you will be able to work successfully below about three hundred feet are very slight, so always leave a safe margin for lining up and landing. As they rise, thermals grow bigger and smoother: close to the ground they can be very rough and display most uncivilised characteristics, so in thermic conditions you must always fly with a reserve of speed, especially when setting up your landing.

The success you have as a thermal-soaring pilot depends on a combination of skill and luck. It will take you much longer to accumulate hours in your logbook than if you were ridge soaring. Although towing techniques are now well established, and infinitely safer than a few years ago, there *are* hazards involved in towing in thermic conditions, and you

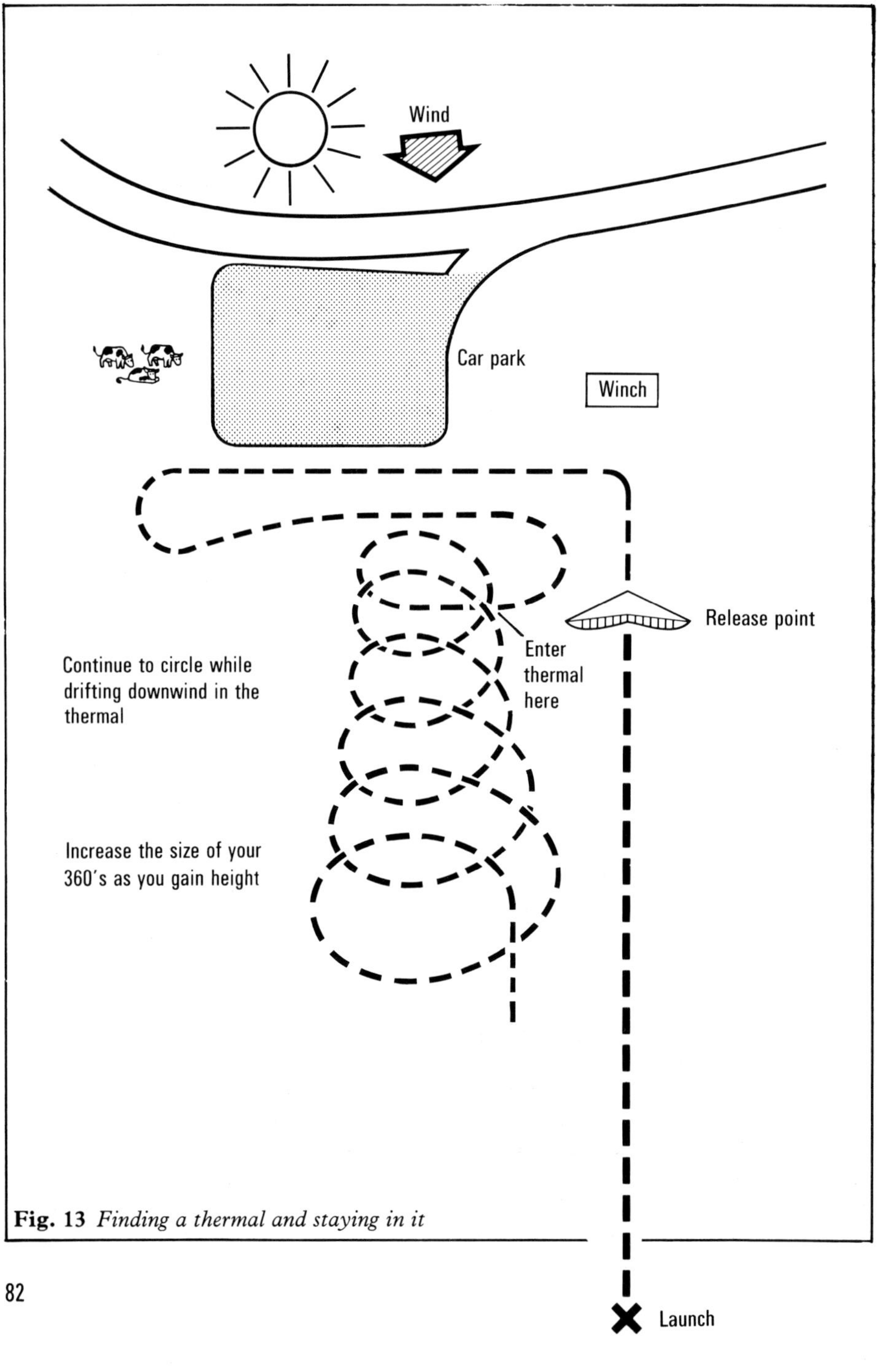


**Fig. 13** *Finding a thermal and staying in it*

must not be so keen to find lift that you are tempted to fly in conditions which you haven't yet got the towline experience to handle.

If your winch is set up on an airfield, you will find that runways are very effective thermal generators: junctions between them seem to work particularly well. If you are extra fortunate you may be launched one summer evening after the runways have been cooking in the sun all day. During the afternoon the strong lift and sink will probably have made it too rough for you to attempt a launch, but towards evening conditions stabilise, and maybe at about 6.00 pm you will release under a cloudless sky, to discover that the vario sounds as strongly after you release as it did on the tow up, and continues to sing wherever you fly. All the air over the airfield feels buoyant. What has happened is that the runways have been soaking up heat all day, and when the ambient temperature drops to a critical level, the air over the runways begins to lift all at once. This is similar to the 'magic lift' effect which ridge fliers occasionally encounter, and if you have the good fortune to find it, you will be able to roam at will over the field without losing height.

## Judging height

I have deliberately not suggested the use of an altimeter at an early stage in your flying experience. Not only is it a distraction at a time when the simple act of flying the glider will be demanding all your attention, but also it is essential that you are able to judge the last couple of hundred feet reasonably accurately without reference to instruments.

I must admit that I know of no way of acquiring this judgement without flying regularly, but if you are taught to tow-launch in a sensible and progressive way, you will not experience any difficulty. You will soon be able to estimate whether there is enough height for a safe 360, a string of S-turns, or if you should just continue straight on into wind for a landing.

Pilots who do most of their flying from tow-launches do not normally have any problem with height judgement, but ridge fliers frequently experience problems when using flat fields for the first time during towing conversion courses.

When you have gained enough experience to be able to control your glider automatically, then by all means invest in an altimeter. Do not buy a cheap one, as altimeters are a classic example of 'yer gets wot yer pays for'. Some of the late-model electronic models give a digital read-out which is accurate to ten feet or less, while the Swiss-made Thommen aneroid instrument indicates to 25 feet and requires no batteries.

## Estimating your touchdown spot

Imagine that you are setting up a landing in a flat field. Wouldn't it be a comfort if you knew where your final glide was going to set you down? Well, here is a simple technique—the 'moving point' system—which will give you a fair indication: with the glider on a good, stable approach glide, select a feature on the ground ahead of you, and without moving

*Judging the landing point. In this case, if the wall appears to be moving downwards in the pilot's field of vision as he approaches it, he will know that he should be able to clear it without difficulty.*

your head, try to assess whether it appears to be moving up or down within your field of vertical vision. If the feature is apparently moving upwards, then your glide will end short of it: if moving downwards, you will overshoot. Once you have decided which applies, you can pick another feature and repeat the exercise until you eventually find a mark which seems to be stationary. You will land very close to that spot. This method won't tell you to a metre where you will touch down, as variations in wind strength as you fly down through the wind gradient will affect the results, as will alterations you make to the glide angle of your aircraft, but it is nevertheless a great help. It does enable you to decide *in good time* which side of a fence to land on, for example.

If you find that you need to shorten your landing distance, rotating your body out of prone will be the greatest help, as the immediate increase in drag will degrade your glide angle considerably. On the other hand, you can stretch the glide by remaining in the prone position and flying as close as you can estimate to the best glide speed of your glider. Best glide will probably occur at about 6 or 8 mph above minimum-sink speed on the average intermediate glider, but this is something you will have to learn to judge for yourself. Don't be misled by diving at high speed towards the ground in an attempt to shorten your landing approach: according to the 'moving point' system you will appear to be going to touch down early, but when you slow down you will regain some altitude.

A variation of the 'moving point' technique can help you to set up your landing directly into wind: when flying straight on your final glide, simply focus on a feature some distance ahead, and watch if it appears to move to left or right. It will soon become automatic to turn slightly and to compensate for the drift in good time.

On this subject of landing directly into wind, do make use of any

external indicators you can find to help you. For a start, you should not have the winch set up without at least one windsock in the field. Get into the habit of keeping an eye on the sock at frequent intervals throughout all your early flights, not just as you start to set up your landing. This will tell you if the wind is swinging around much, and can sometimes give a clue about local turbulence at ground level. Smoke from nearby fields and local buildings is a great help, as are flags and the movement of crops. Even if there is always a windsock where you are learning to soar (and there should be!) it is a good idea to look out for these other indicators as well. One day you will probably be landing-out in strange fields after flying cross-country, and will not have a sock to rely on.

## The Delta bronze badge

You can qualify for the FAI Delta bronze badge from tow-launches. The requirements are:

- Fly 2 km distance over a course with a minimum of 0.5 km between turn points.
- Make five flights with a minimum duration of 5 minutes each.

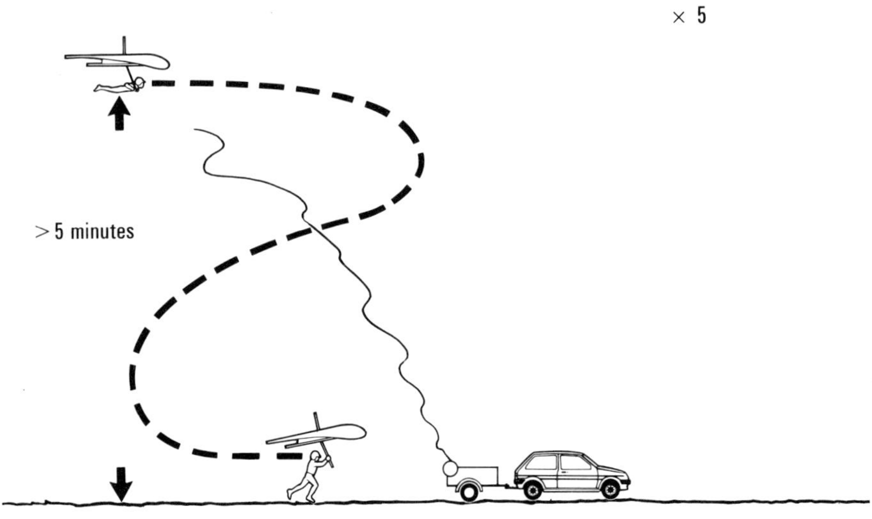


**Fig. 14** *Five flights each of at least five minutes after release*

**Fig. 15** *The 2-km course from a tow launch*

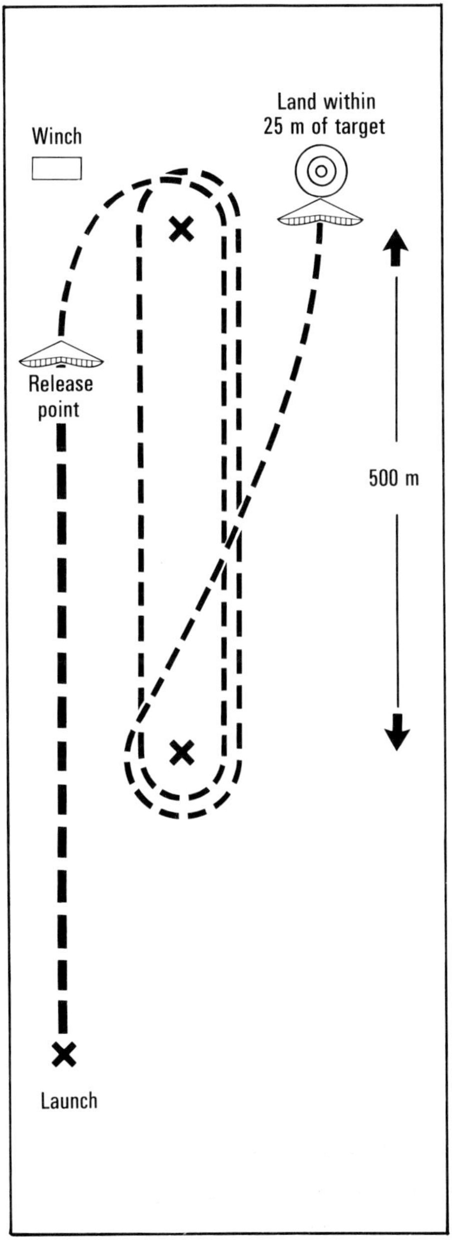


## Checklist

- Concentrate on towline technique so that you achieve a good release height.
- Set yourself accurate patterns to fly.
- Perfect your turns in both directions.
- Don't fly over the line of launch.
- Speed up in sink; slow down in lift.
- Practise height estimation.
- Learn to judge wind direction.

*Flying as close to the hill as this is strictly for the experts! Plenty of speed is essential.*

# Chapter 9
# MOUNTAIN SOARING

## First mountain flights

This chapter is for low-airtime pilots who find they have the opportunity to fly high mountains for the first time.

The idea of making first soaring flights from mountains several thousand feet high will seem a strange one to the average British pilot, yet it is not at all uncommon in alpine areas. Although you do not accumulate air time as quickly as the ridge-soarer, flights of ten or fifteen minutes are easy to achieve, and the hazards are slight if you keep to stable weather conditions and have good local guidance. While I definitely do not reccommend that inexperienced pilots should go chasing off to the mountains at the first possible opportunity, alpine flying is not out of the question once you have become totally reliable at launching and landing, and feel confident in the air.

These tips will make the experience more pleasant:

**1** Have a look at the landing field before you go up the mountain. Check that there is a windsock there, and take particular note of the angle at which the ground slopes. Note local hazards—especially overhead wires of all varieties.

**2** Get a clear idea of where the landing field is, relative to other landmarks, *before* you launch. There's nothing more unnerving than finding that you have 'lost' the field after you are a few minutes into the flight.

**3** Fly an intermediate glider with which you are familiar—don't fall into the trap of thinking that because you are off to special sites it is a good time to get a new glider. You will almost inevitably be making nil-wind landings, and they're not fun at first on a heavy CFX.

**4** Don't expect to fly during the middle of the day, particularly in spring and early summer; wait until the air has settled down towards evening.

**5** Expect to feel nervous the first time you fly towards a field which may be a mile or more distant from take-off. It is not unusual for beginners to leave the launch and fly straight out to the landing field, arriving there a thousand or more feet too high! It would have been better to use some of that precious height to practise a few S-turns or 360's on the way, but if you do end up over the field with a lot of height to lose, decide on a plan and try and stick to it. For example, fly one complete circuit of the field before going to an *upwind* corner where you turn a few gentle steady-speed 360's to use up most of the surplus altitude. Then it's a downwind leg before turning back into wind for landing. Make sure that this final turn takes the form of a wide sweep, and keep plenty of speed on for ease of control.

The flight pattern might look like Fig. 18.

**Fig. 16** *A possible approach pattern in the mountains*

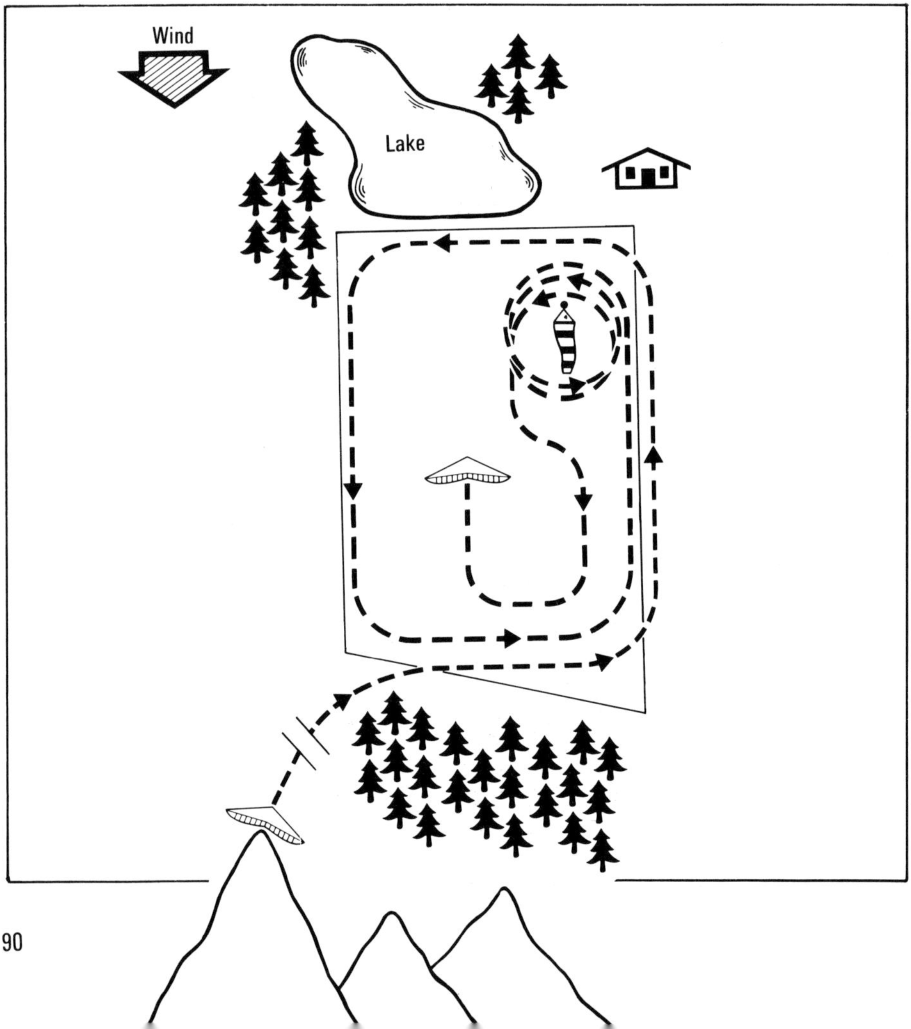

Why don't you do the 360's at the downwind end? That's in case you have underestimated the valley wind; you might then find yourself drifting further downwind and out of range of the field. Naturally, if the air is crowded over the landing field, you must not 'hog' it, but must perform most of your height-losing elsewhere.

Of course, this pattern assumes that you are making your way down into a really large field. If you find that the field looks rather small, and particularly if it is surrounded by trees or other hazards, then the following alternative approach can be useful: however, as a newcomer you should not really be attempting a landing in such a tight spot!

The technique is to track to and fro across the edge of the hazards at the downwind end of the field. (The trees

**Fig. 17** *The best approach to a tight field*

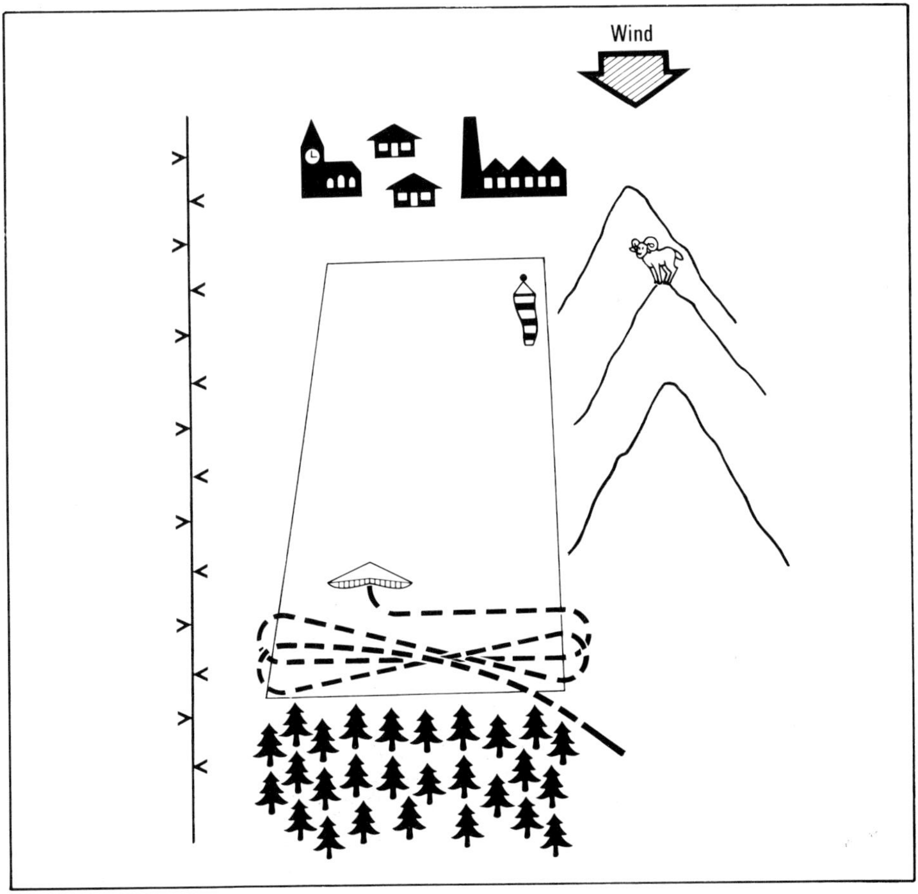

in this case.) You fly *just* in front of them, almost as if they were a ridge you are trying to soar, and as soon as you have lost enough height, you turn out to land. In this sort of situation, try to keep as far away as possible from obstructions at the other end of the field, as there will inevitably be some turbulence. Be sure to fly at a fair speed all the way to your landing flare.

**6** If you haven't yet the skill and confidence to make repeated turns with great precision, don't attempt flights which will require a landing in a tight field.

**7** *Never* allow yourself to get really low over trees during your landing approach. They have an unsporting habit of reaching up and grabbing you!

**8** Give priority to gliders which are lower than you: they always have right of way. This is particularly important when approaching landing fields. Once you are down, clear the middle of the field rapidly to make space for others to land. Bottle up your euphoria until you have carried your glider to the de-rigging area!

**9** *Always* respect local advice.

Flights from top to bottom of a mountain, no matter how big, do not count as soaring unless you manage to work some lift on the way down. Once you are able to handle your glider in air which is occasionally rough, and have learned to S-turn and fly 360's fairly fluently, you can begin to hunt out thermal lift. You need exactly the same skills as the tow-launched pilot: the ability to fly your glider at the appropriate speed, and also to turn it almost instinctively; and you too will need a variometer if you are to make the most of the flying.

## Mountain thermals

If you avoid the strongest thermal conditions, which usually means the height of day during spring and early summer, you can think of extending your airtime by exploring thermal lift quite early in your career. Unfortunately this form of lift is rather elusive at first, and it is easy to stand on the mountain top and imagine that it is pure luck if you happen to find a thermal on your way to the bottom. However, there are ways of improving the odds in your favour. It helps if you think of the thermals as preferring to climb up the sides of mountains rather than just popping up out of the valleys at random. They will also tend to be channelled into gullies, and a spine-backed ridge can have thermals going up both sides of it and converging at the top. Dark patches such as landslips will warm up more than light ones, and south-facing slopes will produce active air earlier than north-facing ones.

Armed with even this slight amount of knowledge, you can begin to extend your flights. For example, after launching, turn and follow the contour of the mountain for some distance; don't be surprised if the variometer tells you that you have found lift as you cross a small gulley, a firebreak or the course of a ski-piste. Try a few S-turns and you may soon be looking down at your takeoff point. Maybe you will gain enough height to fly down directly above a sharp spur of the mountain, which will give you the chance of finding those converging thermals that often supply such powerful lift. Don't let yourself get so carried away that you are tempted into very deep gullies though: they can be impossible to get out of. (One of the most notorious in Austria is known as the 'Bermuda Triangle' for obvious reasons!) Just flying to a very simple plan such as this can make the difference between ten minutes in the air and half an hour.

It is a good idea to take note of a prominent feature further down the mountain, from which you are sure you can reach the landing field, and to use that as your 'break point'. Decide that when you are down to the level of the break point, you will turn out towards the landing field regardless of the chance of finding further lift. This ensures that you do not let yourself become lured out of reach of the field as you hunt for just one more of those elusive thermals!

Treat mountain weather with the greatest respect. If you are used to launching from a smooth British site in winds of 20 mph or more, don't expect to do the same in the Alps. The mountains exaggerate everything: lift is stronger, storms develop more rapidly, wind directions change more quickly, clouds form fast and the turbulence in the lee of mountains can be extreme.

**Note**: Certain countries require visiting pilots to have achieved specified levels of proficiency before making mountain launches. Check before you go. In some European countries a parachute is mandatory.

## Checklist

- Survey the landing area before flying.
- Keep to mellow weather conditions.
- Use your early flights to polish your turning technique.
- Fly a glider you are familiar with.
- Have a simple flight plan and try to stick to it.
- Expect the air to be rough when you do feel confident enough to seek thermals.
- Speed up in sink; slow down in lift.
- Keep out of deep gullies.
- Get local weather advice, and don't take chances with it!

Chapter 10

# INCIDENTS, ACCIDENTS, CRASHES AND TIGHT CORNERS

Are all the tales of doom which the uninformed members of the Great General Public delighted in telling you when you first announced that you were going into the sport, coming true after all? Not at all: hang gliding is the safest of aerial sports, and if you fly with a half-reasonable amount of intelligence, then you won't change that. Modern gliders and safer teaching methods mean that spectacular accidents are virtually unheard of. However, there are moments during those seconds when you make that almost magical transition between ground and air or back again when a little carelessness, inattention or lack of foresight can have painful and expensive consequences: let's look at some of the ways that can happen ...

## Inadequate flare-out

Firstly, you will find yourself having to set up landings in fields and on tracts of moorland which you have not had the previous opportunity of inspecting closely. As you touch down you may discover that you have grossly overestimated the speed with which you can run on that particular piece of ground. If that is the case, then within the next few paces that landing is going to change into a crash.

The sequence of events usually goes something like this:

**1** You enjoy a few good soaring beats in fairly light wind—say about 14 mph.

**2** The wind drops a little, and with it the lift.

**3** You make the correct decision to fly out and down to the bottom-landing field.

**4** Here comes an object lesson in *wind gradient*. There's 4 mph at best down here.

**5** You've used up your available concentration during the soaring part of the flight, and don't work quite as hard as usual at getting your hands nice and high on the control-frame

*For a really positive flare-out you must get your hands high up on the side tubes, as demonstrated by this competition pilot on a Magic. In this case the effort seems to have been made a fraction too soon.*

sides ready for a good flare-out at landing.

**6** Your legs seem to be going like the Road Runner's as you touch down, but still the wing above has enough energy to overtake you!

**7** After a heroic effort you get everything just about under control, but are still moving forward when eventually the wing slows enough to stop flying.

**8** You hang on grimly and will attempt anything to prevent your precious glider from coming in heavily.

**9** The nose of the wing rotates forward and hits the ground. The glider stops with amazing abruptness.

**10** Instinctively you brace yourself by gripping the control-frame uprights as tightly as possible. Your body stops with rather less abruptness than the glider. If you are lucky you will have broken the control frame: without good luck it may be your arm or wrist.

Even though all this happens at walking pace, and a second or so after your feet touch down, it is still a crash. It has happened to most of us at some time or other, and is particularly easy to repeat during your first few flights on a double-surfaced machine. But fortunately the results are rarely as serious as 10 above suggests. The trick is to recognise that your landing is hardly going to be a winner when you are at a point somewhere between 7 and 8 on the list, and to *let go* just before the nose thumps in. The result is always undignified, but at least you are unlikely to hurt yourself.

A variation on the above sequence happens when you leave the flaring-out just a little too late, and the control frame touches down first. The glider stops, but you don't, and again letting go is the best way to minimise damage. The worst that should happen will be some slight bruising of the shoulders where the harness catches them. The chances of your head contacting the keel are slight, but the fact that the chance is there at all is reason enough *always* to wear a good crash helmet when you fly.

It is significant that gliders at training schools have wheels on the bottom bar specifically to avoid landing misjudgements turning into crashes: there is much to be gained by keeping them on for your first few soaring flights at least. In Germany, where Alpine flying frequently involves landing in nil- or switching-wind conditions, the use of wheels by experienced pilots is becoming increasingly common.

If you are tempted to imagine that *you* are strong enough to arrest the forward motion of your body at even quite low speeds by bracing your arms, think how it would feel to stop a full sack of cement swinging into them! And a sack of cement probably weighs less than you do.

## Sloping landing fields

Sloping landing fields have been responsible for wrecking more than their fair share of control frame uprights. You see someone gliding on and on with his glide angle matching that of the ground as the fence at the end approaches. All the wishing in the world won't let him land tidily from three feet high doing twenty miles per hour, and he ends up executing a semi-organised crash in the corner of the field.

What do you do if you find yourself in similar circumstances? Well, by this stage you have a bit of a crisis to handle: if there is really no alternative, all you can do is to come completely out of prone so that your body exerts as much drag as possible and so steepens your glide angle a little. Then slow the glider gently and progressively, using the sort of finesse and concentration required to remove in one piece the foil from the top of a yogurt pot. You are now flying as slowly and as steeply as you can, so just before the fence becomes inevitable, you must flare out with enormous precision and determination. With luck the landing will be a good one: otherwise employ the 'let go' technique outlined above. Because you are slowing down all the time, there is a real danger of stalling and losing control completely—whatever happens, maintain flying speed until the final flare-out.

There are a number of dodges for avoiding the situation: if the landing area undulates, you will do better to land on a relatively steep uphill part, rather than a shallow downhill one. And you will eventually learn just how far off-wind you can land if necessary, but for the time being the sensible option is to choose sites with large safe fields. The mark of a skilled pilot is not to get into tight corners in the first place.

## Landing in an undulating field

Many landing fields, particularly in mountainous or moorland areas, have very irregular surfaces; these demand a special technique which it is as well to know about in advance, even if it takes a bit of practice to perfect. The

*Plenty of hazards here: stone walls, uneven field, turbulence from the trees, plus the danger from the wind-gradient if the pilot gets too close to the hill.*

key to success is always to land on an up-slope, which can mean accelerating down the preceding down-slope with your toes brushing

the ground, and then making a very precisely timed and positive flare as soon as the ground starts rising again. At first it is difficult to keep speed on when so very close to the ground. You also need to have your hands high on the control-frame uprights to give the flare-out the authority it needs.

## Failing to land into wind

Another situation which can have serious consequences is failing to land into wind. Imagine that you are attempting to top-land, and just as you make the final part of your turn, which will bring you fully into wind, a strong gust keeps you turning. You must not for one second relax your efforts to make the glider go the way you require, even if nothing seems to be happening. I know that this sounds elementary, yet it is not uncommon for a novice in this situation to return to the centre of the bar when he feels that his efforts are not achieving the desired effect. The result is inevitably a heavy and potentially very dangerous downwind crash. It is as if the pilot thinks: 'Oh dearie me (and not all pilots are as polite as that), I have lost control, so I will give up at this point and leave the rest of the flight to the glider.' *Don't do it!* Keep the pressure on—many an accident has been turned back into an uneventful touch-down because of the

**A** *Don't even try to land here.*

**B** *Keep reasonable speed between these two points, even if your toes are brushing the grass.*

**C** *Start flare-out here.*

**D** *Easy touch-down here.*

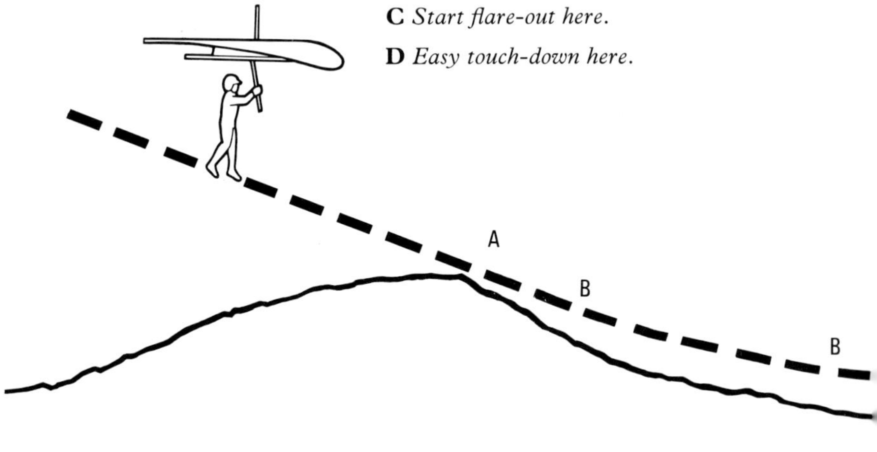


**Fig. 18** *Land on the upslope!*

pilot's efforts in the final metre or so.

Of course, your first duty at all time is to fly safely and uneventfully. For example, in the top-landing incident mentioned here, there would probably have been no drama if the pilot had had another fifty feet of altitude in which to get sorted out. And maybe it was really just a little too gusty or thermic for someone of little experience.

## After touchdown

In stronger winds—particularly at the end of a top landing—immediately you have touched down, get through the control frame and hold onto the front wires to keep the nose of the glider from being blown over backwards. If in any doubt, remain holding on like that until assistance arrives. Otherwise, unclip at the earliest opportunity, and handle the glider by the front wires.

If you find you have to carry a rigged glider any distance in anything above a light breeze, you will find it much easier if you remove the tip-rods (anti-dive rods). Don't forget to re-fit them when you are ready to fly again.

## Launch problems

Bungled launches will naturally lead to accidents, all of them avoidable. Probably the most dangerous mistake

*The pilot of this Atlas has let the nose get too high at the start of his run ...*

*... but he realised in time and pulled-in enough to make a good take-off.*

is failure to get the wings properly level at take-off. Unless positive and instant action is taken by shifting all your weight towards the high wing, it will continue to rise and you will find yourself cartwheeling back into the hill. As in the top-landing example given earlier, you *must* continue to keep the pressure on even when it doesn't seem to be producing the desired effect. On a trip to Germany I saw two gliders wrecked within an hour because the pilots launched badly and appeared to give up at an early stage in the recovery process. In both cases I am confident that the situation was retrievable if the pilots had kept trying.

Mistakes in pitch control at launch can lead you into the sort of situation which can make you wish you had never become a pilot in the first place. Get the nose too high and you will probably take off semi-stalled; until you have increased your flying speed you are at the mercy of the slightest gust. If you allow the nose to get too low, you may next find it slamming down into the ground with amazing abruptness! Both these mistakes usually stem from over-eagerness. Take your time when getting ready for take-off: in all but the very lightest winds, use a wire-man on the nose, but understand that he is there to stop the glider getting out of control, *not* to keep it under control—that's your job. Use an experienced pilot as wire-man: he should show when there is no pressure on the wires by holding on with half-open fingers. When you are confident the wing is properly balanced, and that *you* have control, shout '*Release*', pause a brief moment, and then attack your launch-run.

On very steep sites or cliffs, the brief pause after 'Release' may be either impossible or unacceptably hazardous. However, your first soaring should not generally be attempted from sites which require the special cliff-launch technique: nor should you be setting off into a howling gale. Save such delights until you have built up a bit more experience.

## Light-wind launches

Many experienced pilots find light- or nil-wind take-offs difficult, yet there is a simple dodge which makes them really easy. Here's the secret: *get the wing moving before you do!*

My way is to raise the glider to almost the 'straps-tight' position, but with my hands holding the uprights. Then, without moving my feet, I nudge the wing forward with my shoulders. It immediately becomes natural to start the run a fraction of a second later, slowly at first, and steadily accelerating until you can't stay on the ground any longer.

This system really does work every time; it overcomes the usual problem which arises because you are so obsessed with the need to get up speed that you set off fast and harshly. That almost guarantees that you will out-accelerate the wing and thus let the nose get a bit too high. The resulting extra drag demands extra effort from you, and your chances of a good, clean launch diminish rapidly.

## Wind-gradient dangers

Originally, I was not going to include in this chapter any warnings about the

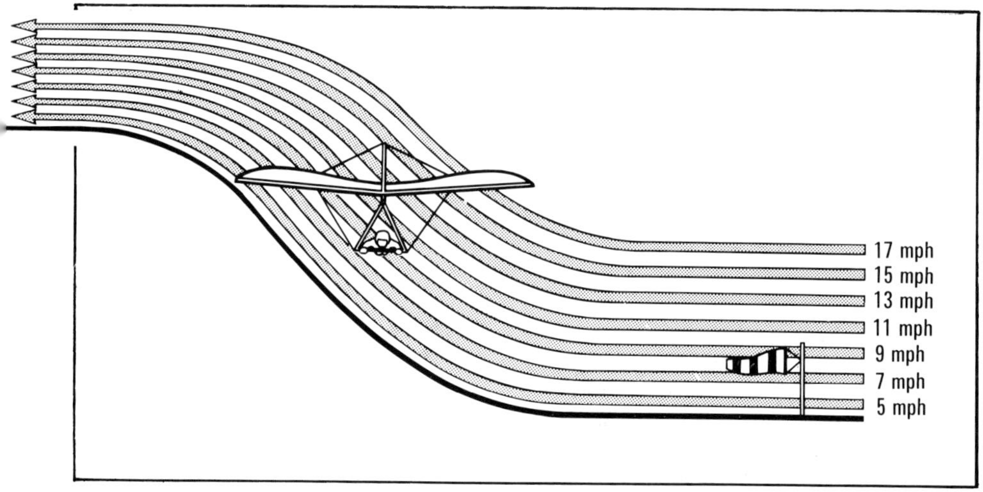

dangers of the wind-gradient when flying close to the hill, because I thought that the subject was covered so fully at the training schools and in all the handbooks. However, when this book was almost ready for press, I saw a young man demonstrate that the art of the stall into the side of a hill is still alive and well, and he is extraordinarily lucky to be the same, so here are the warnings again.

The danger is greatest when you are trying to soar a ridge in light winds, and are below the top. In an attempt to stay up, or at least postpone the moment when it is obvious that your flight is to end in the bottom landing field, you fly at minimum-sink speed with one wing close to the hill. *Wrong!!* Because of the wind-gradient, that wing nearest to the hill will almost inevitably stall in such circumstances, and you will spin in with startling rapidity.

**When flying close to the hill, always keep a surplus of speed in hand.**

I make no apologies for covering the subject of accidents: if it has prevented the odd broken arm or dislocated elbow, then it has been well worth it. Remember, though, that if you do experience a heavy landing or an aborted take-off, a thorough inspection of your glider is essential, to make sure that it hasn't come off worse than you. And fill in a report form—your misfortune could pinpoint a previously overlooked danger which needs publicising.

## Checklist

- Fly defensively, so that incidents won't happen.
- Keep on flying the glider: never give up.
- In light winds, if you've touched down, but are unable to prevent a nose-in: *let go!*
- Too little speed is a far greater danger than too much.
- If you do have an accident, report it!
- Gliders are replaceable, humans are unique.

◄

**Fig. 19** *Never underestimate the wind-gradient effect. If you fly slowly close to the hill like this, the wind gradient will get you sooner or later! The wing nearest the hillside will inevitably stall first, and you will be turned in faster than you can possibly react.*

*The pilot is maintaining concentration over those vital last feet before a top-landing. My personal preference is to have both hands holding the upright at this stage.*

## Chapter 11
# SUMMING UP

Soaring is simply a matter of keeping your glider in lifting air.

You won't stay in lifting air if you cannot fly your aircraft accurately and efficiently, so master this before trying to soar.

Get competent with your equipment, particularly the prone harness, at an early stage: resist the temptation to think that if you can just get high in the sky, everything will somehow miraculously sort itself out all at once.

If at all possible, start out on a good intermediate glider, or one of the latest models which are made especially for new soaring pilots.

Take the time to go to the best possible site for your first soaring experience, and go with a really reliable and experienced pilot. Clubs are beginning to organise special 'introduction to soaring' days, and some schools offer soaring courses. In either case you can be confident that you will be given sound advice.

Learn at *your* speed, and don't be afraid to ask for advice.

Join a club. Not only will this bring you into contact with many pilots who are more experienced, but you will also find that there are lots more at the same stage as yourself with whom to compare notes.

If you are learning from tow launches, make a special effort to extend your skills on each flight, rather than repeating exactly the same circuit. Consider taking a hill-launching endorsement course so that you can gain airtime from hillsides too.

Always have a large part of your brain tuned in to the safety wavelengths: glider safety, site safety, weather safety and personal flying safety.

Enjoy every minute of it all!

# USEFUL ADDRESSES

**British Hang Gliding Association (BHGA)**
Cranfield Airfield
Cranfield
Bedfordshire
MK43 0YR

Bedford (0234) 751688

**British Association of Parascending Clubs (BAPC)**
18 Talbot Lane
Leicester
LE1 4LR

Leicester (0533) 530318

**British Gliding Association (BGA)**
Kimberley House
Vaughan Way
Leicester
LE1 4SG

Leicester (0533) 531051

**Civil Aviation Authority (CAA)**
CAA House
45-59 Kingsway
London
WC2B 6TE

01-405 6922

**Fédération Aéronautique Internationale**
10–12 Rue du Capitaine Menard
75015 Paris
France

---

*Titles marked with an asterisk are available by mail order from White Line Press, 60 Bradford Road, Stanningley, Leeds LS28 6EF. Please write for an up-to-date price list.

# FURTHER READING

*Noel Whittall, *The Complete Hang Gliding Guide*, (A & C Black)

'An up-to-date tell-all textbook for the complete novice or the more experienced pilot. Lavish colour illustrations. The best in its class.' [*Sky Lights*]

*BHGA Student Handbook*, (BHGA)

*BHGA Pilot Handbook*, (BHGA)

Absolutely essential reading for all British pilots: full information on air law, flying safety and much more.

*Derek Piggott, *Understanding Flying Weather*, (A & C Black)

The most practical weather book ever published for British pilots. The information is completely relevant to hang gliding, and the style makes it easy to understand this complex subject. Highly recommended.

Bob Mackay, *An Introduction to Hang Gliding*, (Thornhill Press)

A no-nonsense readable guide; very good value.

Dennis Pagen, *Flying Skills*, (Dennis Pagen)

Dennis Pagen, *Techniques (Advanced Pilots)*, (Dennis Pagen)

Dennis Pagen, *Flying Conditions*, (Dennis Pagen)

Published in the USA, but most of the contents are international. The widest range of technical information available on flex-wing flight. Very good books to keep coming back to.

Ann Welch & Roy Hill, *Soaring Hang Gliders*, (John Murray)

Some good soaring information, but this book became dated sooner than it deserved.

*Wings!* magazine

Published monthly by the BHGA. The staple diet for all followers of the sport.

# INDEX